Uneasily Yoked

By Kiara A. Johns

Foreword: Robert Johns
Editor: Nicholas Wolak

ISBN: 978-1-7341948-4-5

First Edition

Preeminent Publishing Co.
www.KiaraAJohns.com

Table of Contents

Dedication

This book is dedicated to God (Yahweh), the lover and keeper of my soul. To Jesus Christ (Yahshua), my Lord and Savior; and to the Holy Spirit, my comforter. Thank you for keeping me, when I did not deserve to be kept. You've always been my protector, provider, deliverer and redeemer; Therefore, with this life you have given me, I will serve you forever. Let thy will be done.

Acknowledgements

I would like to thank Robert Johns, the man who protects, provides, and covers our family. The one who prays for me continuously, loves me despite my past, and encourages me to run towards my future. For you I am forever grateful to God. I'm so blessed to share this life with you. I love you forever.

Thank you to my family. My parents April and Gabriel McCullum, who tirelessly encourage me to serve God and seek after the plan he has for my life, rather than my own. My siblings, Kelan, Tiana, Jay'vone, Mildred and Kendra. Words cannot describe the love and gratitude I have for you; Thank you all for loving me despite my flaws.

I would also like to thank the ladies of Victory House Transitional Center for Girls. My sisters, you all helped change my life and gave me hope in a desperate time. Thank you all for teaching me how to love from selflessness. Yolanda, I am forever grateful for your presence in my life. You are forever my hero, forever my little sister.

To Shilah Vaughn, thank you for always being my best friend. Through the good bad and ugly, you're always around. I love you.

To Nicole John -You have wiped innumerable tears from my eyes, you've fed me when I was too weak to feed myself. Regardless of how near or far we are in distance or in heart, nothing can change the impact of your presence in my life. I love you despite our differences. You are and forever will be my best friend, my sister, and my person.

To "The very nice woman, extremely beautiful and well spoken", Thank you for your transparency and for allowing God to use you, in order for me to receive deliverance. May you one day, find your "Promise".

To Nich Wolak - you're the bomb! Thanks for making this editing experience so much fun. I appreciate your time and your skillset.

Lastly, I would like to thank anyone that has ever prayed for me, supported me, and encouraged me. I pray for God's continued blessing and favor over your life.

Foreword

I met Kiara at Ferris State University in 2010. We were both active leaders on campus and members of brother/sister organizations. We established a very close connection around Summer 2011/2012.

In the last 8 years I have been able to witness what Kiara testifies about in her writing. I was able to witness her thoughts, actions and reactions to most of the events she writes about while they were taking place. As a result, I can attest to the fact that in each situation that she wound up in, she never thought she was settling. She always looked for the best in every person and sought to understand them and their circumstances which caused her to turn blind eye to some things that may have seemed obvious from the outside. This may have even caused her to unconsciously lower her standards that she had set for herself and anyone else who was trying to be in a certain space in her life.

The end result: her fair share of unequally yoked relationships. Each of them came with their own set of consequences: damage to reputation, soul ties, abuse, humiliation and trauma. Collectively, each encounter had one thing in common: spiritual destruction. She is a witness to how easy it is to become entangled in such a relationship but how difficult it is to disconnect and move forward. Even though she is and has always been a believer, she can attest to how she tried to make these relationships work although they were against God's word.

Over the years, she has grown both spiritually and emotionally as a woman. She has come to terms with the errors of her actions, admitted her wrongdoings and strived to learn and evolve from them. These experiences have increased her effectiveness as a minister of the Gospel, especially as it pertains to ministering to women of all ages about their devotion to Christ while waiting for a mate.

Kiara is and has always been a mentor for young women and an advocate for women's rights and equality. So, it is fitting of her to author a book that tells her story and exposes her dreadful past all in hopes to empower women to know their worth and never settle for anything short of what God has for them, especially as it pertains to a man.

In this book Kiara, details her experiences like never before. As one of her best friends, who was always around, there are some things in the pages of the book that I didn't even know until around the time I became her husband. She equips the reader to avoid unequally yoked relationship and how to identify if they are in one. Most importantly, she provides the key and subsequent steps to dissolve an unequally yoked relationship.

This book is especially relevant in today's society as many are looking for love at the wrong times and in all of the wrong places. Some are settling and compromising their standards. Others are in situations that they don't want to be in but have no idea how to get out. Her writing serves as a perfect example on how easy it is to become that woman that you said that could never be you or end up in a situation that you said you could never end up in. Kiara, like many women today never signed up from the beginning to be humiliated, abused, stalked or hurt. Instead, they were seeking to be loved and to be fulfilled. However, when the situation turned into that thing that they didn't sign up for they had a hard time separating from the person who they had such high expectations and hopes for. So, the options then appear to be to lower the standard or risk the happiness that they sought out for. Too many women chose the easier option to lower their standards.

Kiara makes it clear in sharing her experiences that no matter how many times you fall, get back up. Victory can only be gained by getting back into the fight. If you stay down, you are destined for defeat and in the case of the believe destined to be outside of the will of God.

I know that Kiara would agree that if she had just fully submitted to God in the first place, aligned herself to his will and waited for him, she would have avoided all of the hurt and pain she experienced up until her happy ending that God had always had planned for her.

Chapter One: World Series

"It's got to be that can't-eat, can't-sleep, reach-for-the-stars, over-the-fence, World Series kind of stuff, right?

-Mary-Kate Olsen

Chapter One: World Series

In 1995 there was a film released called, “It Takes Two”, starring Kirstie Alley, Steve Guttenberg and Mary-Kate and Ashley Olsen. The movie is centered around twin girls who were separated at birth. By happenstance they meet at summer camp and plot to make their caregivers fall in love with one another. Kirstie Alley plays Diane, a social worker with dreams of adopting Amanda (Mary-Kate). Her reasons for not adopting are due to money, and the belief that children deserve to be in two-parent households, which leads to the following conversation between her and Amanda:

Amanda: So adopt me, why don't you!

Diane: They won't let me adopt you on my salary; besides, you deserve a mother *and* a father.

Amanda: So, get a husband.

Diane: It's not like buying a car, you know.

Amanda: I know. It's got to be that can't-eat, can't-sleep, reach-for-the-stars, over-the-fence, World Series kind of stuff, right?

Diane: Hey, a girl's got to have her standards.

This might be my earliest memory of hearing an expression of what love is supposed to be. I was five years old when the movie was released, but it was only the beginning of my understanding of love and family dynamics. My understanding and imagination concerning love subconsciously went downhill from this point on, or possibly even before. What I do know is that this would become one of my favorite movie quotes. For years I quoted this movie to my sisters, friends and romantic partners concerning what the standard of love should be. This became the lens through which I viewed every relationship, whether it was my own, or others. This view I gleaned, that love was an over-the-top fairy tale, which required great sacrifice, broken rules and tears was not only superficial, but also very dangerous.

I have never been a stranger to love stories, notes, songs and movies. The idea of love being a fairy tale reaches all the way back to my childhood. Somehow the idea that love and pain must coexist in a romantic relationship became normal to me. I remember being a young woman watching the movie "Love and Basketball," in awe of Quincy (Omar Epps) and Monica's (Sanaa Lathan) love story. I credit that film for sparking my interest in losing my virginity, as for me it introduced an age (or moreso grade) that was deemed socially appropriate to begin having sex; It placed an expectation on prom night.

As a young girl, I watched this movie many times reciting the conversation between Quincy and Monica concerning his choice for a prom date, and how Shawnee Easton (Gabrielle Union) had bargained, that if he took her to the prom, she would leave him satisfied. Although Quincy would take her to prom, he would not end the night romantically with Shawnee, but rather by taking Monica's virginity. Shawnee may have not been Qunicy's main choice for a girlfriend, but she certainly gained his attention. The key factor in Quincy identifying Shawnee was her body. This movie and Shawnee Easton made me embrace my physique, before then I had been ashamed of my breasts; but the very attribute I was hiding, is what Shawnee used to attract boys. I wanted to be like Shawnee Easton and attract my own Quincy.

"Love and Basketball" was also the spark of interest for my desire to marry someone who I'd known since childhood. As much as I was intrigued by Shawnee, I also admired Monica. Monica had something that I desired- A fairy-tale ending. Although her victory did not come without battle, she eventually went on to marry Quincy. This story and the many other urban fairytales like it come with pain, betrayal, sexism and a faint glimpse of what love entails. I became infatuated with the idea that longevity and the amount of trials a couple overcame outweighed doing it the right way. I had already accepted that heartbreak comes with the territory of love, even before I was of age to date. Yet deep down inside of me, there was a faint hope that perhaps everyone else had done it wrong.

I've always wanted that reach for the stars, over the moon, World Series kind of love. The love that was created in the heavens and birthed into our lives in the most simplistic ways. That can't eat, can't sleep, let's fall asleep on the phone, I need to hear your heartbeat next to mine love. I am a hopeless romantic, constantly daydreaming about the perfect wedding, naming my children, and imagining myself washing dishes as my husband comes home for a perfect dinner.

For years I've been fascinated with love and its many strengths; silently obsessing over the fabricated feelings its counterfeits provide. With each encounter I hope to be one step closer to its most genuine and purest form. Heartbreak after heartbreak I prayed that next time would be my time; as I mustered enough energy to wipe the tears from my face. I've sat through countless weddings, smiling and praying no one asked me where my date was; or even worse, "Would I be next to get married?" Each time was like a jab to the abdomen. I would fight back tears and jokingly respond that I wasn't down for it, hoping that if people felt as if I wasn't interested in marriage; it wouldn't give the impression that I wasn't desired for marriage.

I'm not exactly sure how I came to this point. What happened to create the void inside of me that made me feel as though I lacked character or quality due to my singleness? Somehow, I had been overtaken with an emptiness, and each time I would lose more of myself than before. I would hold my phone, contemplating whether to unblock them. I would reason with myself as to whether my verbally abusive atheist boyfriend would ever find a relationship with God, challenging myself that perhaps I was supposed to be a light guiding him to Christ.

In lust, I would send nude pictures to a man, who would later share them with the world. I would measure the likelihood of whether my married boyfriend was ever going to get a divorce. There was no specific gauge on where I met these men, nor was one relationship better than another; they all ended in disaster. Whether we met in high school, social dating apps, or in church, each of them were perfect in their ability to shake up my life and leave me questioning my morals.

Still I would contemplate, weighing the options that perhaps the temporary comfort was better than the hurt that currently ached my heart. To say that I felt miserable and pathetic was an understatement; but each time I went back in for love. For the moment, love letters, roses, dinner and the lies told to keep me smiling were enough to keep me around and in high spirits, until the reality of those relationships set in. I used to pride myself on having certain standards and expectations. I wasn't what some might call a serial dater. I wasn't easy and I could count the number of relationships I've had, most of which were long term.

I would make myself believe I was on the right track because I would never entertain the type of men other women (including some of my friends) would. I had no problem requiring men to treat me well, buy me things or take me out. I was never hidden, and I made it crystal clear that I was the prize, yet while my words conveyed these things, I still found myself to be in compromising positions. I thought that because I dated a "different type" of man - those who could be described as being more socially and spiritually aware or conscious - I would be exempt from heartbreak, and that our relationship was more meaningful.

In hindsight, every relationship I entered would be a catalyst to assist in the destruction of my self-worth. It would progressively get worse as the years, and relationships passed. I would meet different men, fall in love, and later realize the issues we really faced that made it impossible for us to coexist in love were spiritual, rather than physically- and emotionally-based. It was a long time before I took the advice, I gave others, about not settling for less than what God has ordained to be best for you. This is something I still struggle with, perhaps not in relationships, but in other life challenges. Many times, I've tried to place men, friends, experiences and situationships in the forever box, and God had to forcefully remove them by showing me what my future would be like with them.

This experience can be scary. Honestly, it was more like self-inflicted torment, because I knew the right things to do. As much as Hollywood had planted a superficial ideal of what love is inside my head, I had experienced love in its purest form. I knew God to be the ultimate love, and in my heart, I wanted a man to love me with the love of Christ. I wanted a marriage, with children, and to submit to my husband as unto the Lord. I deeply desired for a husband to love me as Christ loved the church. The irony was I went everywhere but to God to find a representation of his love. It would be years before I realized that my problem was not physical, it was not with men, it wasn't with anyone but myself.

If you have experienced this and you're anything like me, it may have invoked a rebellious feeling inside of you that said, "No… this is what I deserve and I'm going to get it! I had to learn that, apart from God's perfect will, everything stood to be circumstantial and out of his ark of safety. I would bump my head many times on this struggle to submit (Don't we all hate that word?!?) to God's plan in my life. I'd question God and those around me on why these things (or these men) kept happening to me. I say that these men happened to me, because I believe that I played a large role in their lives spiritually, whether I have yet to see it manifest or not. It was not by coincidence or mistake that I met them, or that our bonds formed. In no way am I saying that God told me to have premarital sex with, covet, or trust them with my heart. What I would like to express is that each of these men shed light on who I was, and where I was, spiritually at the time that I met them.

As Christians we tend to overestimate where we are in our walk with God, or our strength to face temptation. This can be detrimental to those that we are dating because a lapse in our character, or standards, can prove to be deadly both physically and spiritually. I often speak to young women who are in relationships where they are unequally yoked with their partner. For many of my peers, the idea of dating someone who is not a believer, or actively pursuing their faith in the same manner that you are, does not pose an issue. This is partially because the implications of this are not understood until much later, when our souls are tied to spirits that are facing torment, and we are left praying for a way out.

The term "equally yoked" is a biblical phrase that explains the moral standard in a relationship and/or marriage. The scripture reference is 2 Corinthians 6:14-18 (KJV) where it reads:

Be ye not unequally yoked together with unbelievers: for what fellowship hath righteousness with unrighteousness? and what communion hath light with darkness? And what concord hath Christ with Satan (Belial)? or what part hath he that believeth with an infidel? And what agreement hath the temple of God with idols? for ye are the temple of the living God; as God hath said, I will dwell in them, and walk in them; and I will be their God, and they shall be my people. Wherefore come out from among them, and be ye separate, saith the Lord, and touch not the unclean thing; and I will receive you. And will be a Father unto you, and ye shall be my sons and daughters, saith the Lord Almighty.

This scripture passage gives insight on why it is important for a believer to not be yoked with an unbeliever, by posing questions which lead the reader to consider their sharp contrast concerning morals and standards of life. The most vivid comparison would be of light and darkness, which as believers we know to be a representation of good and evil. When we are unequally yoked in a relationship, we can never effectively accomplish the purpose that God has set out for us to do, because we are at odds with the person who should be striving to become one flesh with us. This means that the very person who your purpose and future is supposed to be entrusted to is also an enemy. Your beliefs don't align, and your spirits are at odds with one another.

Imagine being deeply wounded or injured, in dire need of medical attention and you cannot make it into the emergency room without the assistance of the person you're attached to. As you are attempting to walk toward the door, the person you have chosen to walk with is pulling you in the opposite direction. Whether knowingly or unknowingly because they don't see, understand, accept, or agree with your need, you are going without the medical attention you need to survive. Being unequally spiritually yoked is the same way. Any time we create a covenant with a person outside of God's will, we hinder our ability to go to him and get the attention we need to survive, or even thrive, in this world.

The idea of being unequally yoked comes from the yoking of oxen. A yoke is a wooden plank that is harnessed around the necks of two oxen in efforts to share pulled weight. Together yoking two oxen enables them to pull two times their body weight, averaging between 6,000 and 12,000 pounds, yet this can only occur when they are equally yoked, equally yoked in size, strength and stature. When they are not matched properly, they too are unable to fulfill the task that is before them and they often wander in circles or move at different paces, the stronger one dragging the slower party, the couple unable to operate at its full potential.

Oh, I never thought I'd have so many similarities to an ox. Yet on many occasions and in many friendships, relationships and situationships, I've linked myself to people who just weren't ordained to take this faith walk with me. If I were to be 100-percent honest, most of these people were not ordained to go anywhere with me, let alone into my purpose, but somehow, I held on to them. Just like that ox, I wandered aimlessly in circles.

Chapter Two: An Ode to Pain

"Well I'm not gon cry,
I'm not gon cry,
I'm not gon shed no tears
No, I'm not gon cry,
it's not the time
cuz you're not worth my tears"

-Mary J. Blige

Chapter Two: An Ode to Pain

For as long as I can remember, movies, music, and media have always been a part of my life. I grew up in the '90s, listening to the sweet soulful sounds of Mary J. Blige, as she sang "Real Love." Well before I was able to identify with the pain from which she sang "Not Gon' Cry," I remember belting all the lyrics from memory. I also rapped Lil Kim's verse on "I Can Love You" as if I was in concert.

By the time the 2000s approached, I was deep into the Murder Inc Era; Ja Rule and Ashanti's music videos had all the young women wanting to be a "Down A** Chick," to defy the rules and their self-worth in the name of love. Through these outlets (and probably many other planted seeds), I became acquainted with the idea that pain is love. It became all-too familiar and natural for me to expect the mistakes and mistreatment of men and boys alike. I had been desensitized to this behavior; it was normal to me. I had embraced the mantra, "Any Love worth having is worth fighting for, that a true love will make it through the hardest challenges. It was a badge of honor to say, "We made it through hardship and turmoil and came out stronger."

But I'd later have to ask myself, "Why is it necessary to weaken my spirit to create a stronger bond of infatuation with someone who mistreats me?" I'd question where this obsession with pain stemmed from, how it enabled me to accept some of the most volatile behavior. Somehow, I had figured out a way to wrap it in the word love.

I never knew that love was not supposed to hurt. The idea that love was beautiful, joyful and painless was foreign. I watched women in the media and my life lessen their voices, spirits and light to embody a love and life less than what God had ordained for them. I remember my mother telling me, "You have to go through something with someone. You just have to decide who you're willing to go through it with." I incorporated the ideal that pain came with the territory of love. This often led me to fall into the traps of Satan, distracting me from my true purpose.

And oh, how I loved those distractions! They often arrived just to my liking, tall, dark and handsome, with nice teeth. They came with lips equipped to give smooth kisses and whisper sweet words. Their hands were helpful enough to drown me in sin.

Pain, what I once believed to be the counterpart of love, I later found out that the two were mutually exclusive rather than mutually inclusive. Yet before I was able to understand that pain and love did not coexist, I accepted them as the same. Unaware that the longer I entertained pain, It would prolong my encounter with love.

Pain was indeed my distraction, and I simultaneously hated and loved everything about you. At the time you were everything I could imagine and everything I've ever dreamed. Often too perfect to be untrue, yet so far from being real. It was so hard for me to grasp the reality of their untimely and even more uncommon presence. It's difficult to interpret and accept the surreal ambience that they projected. Even the tears they made me cry were sweet. The smiles that they brought gave temporary relief from my agony, giving me life during dysfunction and luring me into my darkest days. Many days I sat with tears streaming down my face, and I could feel my heart pulsating through my chest. Each heartbeat brought a sense of mortality that shattered a part of me that what I once thought was invincible.

In that same moment I'd also feel an increased mental capacity, self-awareness, and bravery. Therefore, I fought for you; even when I doubted your existence and I felt alone in every aspect of my life. It was my hope that your true existence would one day come into my life. The idea of you often saved me from self-destruction, revitalizing my spirit, rejuvenating my mind and pushing the blood through my veins.

You gave me encouragement, and even after finding you, I'm amazed at your thriving passion in seeking yourself whether in words, deeds or in others. On my search for you I learned that you are reckless indeed, going into the deepest of depths, and the darkest of nights to reach those you love, as counterfeits, other gods, philosophers, and the agnostic intellectual mind reason with your ideals. If Plato was correct in his theory - that we were once whole beings that have been split into halves and are now doomed to roam the earth, desperately in search of our other halves - know that I too shared in your sorrow of being unable to reconnect. I rejoice in the thought of you. I'm pained by our separation and disgusted by the idea of a mere imitation.

Throughout the years I constantly found myself pondering about my future, hopelessly realizing that you may not be a part of it, that we may never create life and build legacy. I am sure we are similar in many ways, believing in the possibility of each other, yet trapped by a world that makes it more difficult for us to encounter one another.

I've searched for you in many books, inside of poetry, movies, songs and hobbies. I've danced with imitations and slept with your viciously fraudulent counterparts. I've screamed and laughed. I've cried and mourned for the loss of ones who I surely thought you'd be. We've taken shots of tequila and danced. I've been drunk and cried to you and for you. I've gazed into someone's eyes and perhaps caught a mere glimpse of your purity. We've been through it all, yet still one thing remains consistent and that's your inconsistency.

You come and you leave. Everything is perfect when you're around, yet when you exit you destroy a part of me every time. At times I wish to never know you again; then that very thought is erased by a flood of thoughts consisting of my wrongdoing and what I'll do better next time. All I know for sure is that when you leave you never bow out gracefully; you always go out with a bang. You go straight for the jugular, in hopes of destroying all things vital. You leave the bedroom, kitchen and living room in shambles, pictures torn from frames, plans, routines, hopes and dreams shattered. I don't sleep for days, hoping that you'll walk back through the door and fix everything that you've broken.

I've wished so many times that I could just close my eyes and wish away the discomfort and void that was left. I've toughed it out and pretended to be fine, until time took away your memories. I wish for nothing more than to forget the heartache and agony, yet I open the door every time you knock. Whoever you are, wherever we are, I always give you my best. I give you my all hoping that you come along and revitalize my life and energize my spirit.

Truthfully, I don't know who you are. I'm searching for proof that you are worth it and because of this I'm content with the idea that you're not a person. I question rather I have been called, just as the apostle Paul was, to a life of singleness. I am growing content with the idea that the only love I may encounter, will be of God. Adopting the things that I lack and the freedoms I desire - things that will never be - I live vicariously through the idea that love is inside of me. Where you have failed, I will succeed in loving. To believe that pure love exists beyond one's self is such a risk and this investment hasn't brought forth fruit and has shown to not accumulate in value. It decreases over time and its tangible and non-tangible assets become less. Surely love has proven to be a liability. I'm not damaged, I'm not angry, nor am I rebellious against the rules. What I am is oblivious to the ones that loved me too.

So, where are you? Cause today we break up. I think maybe we should just be friends, perhaps that's not even a good idea. Let's not be anything.

Because I have longed for you and I am beginning to feel as though you are unattainable. I can't feel you and I can't see you visibly present in anything that surrounds me. This is from a dark and lonely place, a place that desires your shine and that the glory of you is birthed into everything that surrounds me. What am I? What have I done wrong? What are the errors of my ways? Am I trapped by past mistakes? I'm angry because I have always wanted you, yet I've always been denied your security.

In your name, A boy I liked once told me he loved me … before he cursed my god and disrespected my faith and my body.

In the name of love, a guy I wanted once tried to own me. He wanted a possession, just another to add to his collection, to control me. He violated my space, shared my secrets and created a fear inside of me.

For you, I chose a man who once told me I wasn't the kind of woman to be a side piece or baby momma. He never told me he loved me, but that he cared too much to ruin my life. He told me that I was a wife … and he wasn't in a place to love me the way I deserved. He said he was young and exploring who he wanted to become and where he wanted to go in life. He told me he didn't want to hurt me, but that he would never let me be with someone who didn't appreciate me the way I deserved to be. His inconsistency ultimately ended us, and for someone who didn't want to hurt me, that's exactly what he did.

Another left me empty and unhopeful. My heart bruised. My mind wandering. My spirit restless. He's left me jealous, confused, angry with myself and with God. He's become my why, my question of God's reasoning. He became my prayer. He was the shattered pieces of my heart frozen in place, waiting to be thawed and mended together again.

He was my headache, my heartache. The thorn in my flesh. A self-reflection or mirror of disappointment. Yet perhaps he was the miracle that saved me from myself. The sacrifice that keeps me for the next heart that's meant to love me.

Somewhere deep in my mind or heart I'm grateful; I just need to find that place amid the anguish. The strength and muscle to shrug. The ability to shake the desire to make them all eat their words and look back with regret. Healing, perhaps that's a better description of what I need. Somewhere inside me there is a woman, healed and capable of loving and trusting blindly. One who believes in fairy tales and happy endings … I just don't know how to get back to her.

Chapter Three: Fool Me Twice...

"BLAME IT ON ME
Say it's my fault
Say that I left you outside in the cold with a broken heart
I really don't care
I ain't crying no more
Say I'm a liar a cheater
Say anything that you want
As long as it's over"

-Chrisette Michelle

Chapter Three: Fool Me Twice…

Chrisette Michelle released a song on her 2009 album "Epiphany" called "Blame it on Me." I remember being in my bedroom the first time I heard it in April 2011. I cried myself to sleep as I struggled with the back and forth of my first relationship. The song wasn't new at the time, but I had never heard it before that day. The song awoke me from my sleep in the early hours of the morning as it radiated through the speakers. The beautiful sounds that came from Chrisette Michelle's voice, told of a painful relationship and the woman's frustration and desperate desire to be released. Freedom was what she wanted, and the innermost parts of my soul could identify. I had been dating my high school sweetheart, Darrin (*Editor's Note: Most names have been changed) on and off for the last four years, and the relationship had hit its climax. The thought of who was at fault was no longer important.

Has anyone ever hurt you so bad that by the time it was over, you could not hold any hate or animosity toward them? So bad you were relieved to be free from the pain of having to love them, grateful for your way of escape? I was in a relationship that hurt me so bad I almost had no desire to live. I hated him for not being the person, he had promised me to be. He had vowed to remain the same respectful, gentle character that he portrayed himself to be upon our introduction, but that soon changed for the worse. I had reached the point where I could not see an end to the pain I was feeling and I could not imagine a life beyond the one I currently had, I could not let go of the plans we had built.

To make matters worse, I was letting the relationship go for God. I remember him telling me I was crazy (and me feeling as if I was crazy) to give up a relationship with a man who loves me, for a God that I couldn't see, and that he felt I couldn't prove existed. Nonetheless, when the relationship finally ended and God opened my eyes to who I was in conjoined with, I was disappointed with myself for the years of my life wasted, yet grateful to God for the lessons I had learned. I went on to search for the purpose in which God created me, but not without that test, the test of who and what I would stand for, circling back. After the dust of this relationship settled, I eventually moved on with my life and transitioned into finding the things I loved. I progressed into who I truly wanted to become, but not without repeated failures of trying to force unequally yoked relationships. I would have never guessed that after leaving this relationship, I would subconsciously seek and recreate the same scenario with different men.

I'm sure it started off as puppy love and grew into something that I'm still not able to classify, but if I had to think of a word to summarize the experience it would be obsession. I wouldn't go to the extent to say I was obsessed with him, but with the idea of love, thus I attempted to make it work by any means necessary. In retrospect, I question if I ever was in love or whether I was attracted to the mere thought of what love could be. Regardless, I willingly gave my heart away and allowed it to be disrespected in so many ways. I invested all of me into this relationship from the start, after all it was my first real encounter with love. On the scale of Ike and Tina Turner to Steph and Ayesha Curry, we were somewhere around Tom Cruise and Katie Holmes, with a hint of Chris Brown and Rhianna (minus the fame and millions of dollars).

We were very young, immature and toxic to each other lives, yet I'm sure he would agree that we took the relationship very seriously. As much as he was dark, my light wasn't strong enough, nor my character bold enough to stand steadfast on God's truths and draw him out. My desire for him most often outweighed my commitment to hold to who I knew God wanted me to become. I would often allow my flesh or lustful attractions to detour me from his plan.

We were sixteen and seventeen - high school sweethearts - and what started out so simple became so complex in a matter of seconds, forcing me to make very adult decisions. As it most often goes, it was perfect when we were kids. Our teenage love affair was the epitome of all love stories. Darrin and I shared that "can't eat, can't sleep, walk you home from school every day, plan our lives out together, let's get married young and grow old" type of love. And if you haven't guessed by now, I use the word love very loosely. We were everything to each other and we did everything.

I was the editor of the yearbook, president of student council and DECA (an organization for future leaders in marketing, finance, hospitality and management), and an executive board member for our senior class. Darrin was captain of the football team and I wore his jersey to the football games.

We had been friends for three years, and our senior year we decided to date. That year we were also nominated and ran for class couple and homecoming king and queen. We were so in love, and we made promises that neither one of us could keep, promises to love and respect each other forever - we both failed miserably. At times I feel as if I should have ran to the nearest exit on the day that we met, or changed my class schedule. I'd be lying to say that this isn't an experience that I regret, I do. It was a life lesson, one that I wish that I had never had to learn. While I understand that in my present all things work together for my good (Romans 8:28), I realize that had I been obedient to the word and the will of God, I would not have experienced the same turmoil.

I was so committed to making this work, because it was the fairy tale that I thought I always wanted. In my mind this was the perfect start to a great life. We made plans to one day have children, marry, start a business, and further our education together. I had always wanted to save myself for marriage. On Jan. 26, 2007 I gave up on that desire. After all, I loved him, and we had plans. In the fall the both of us would be attending the same university and moving in the right direction towards our happily ever after.

It's funny how often adults can see things in your life that you can't as a child. I was told that he was bad for me since Day 1. Teachers, parents, friends and mentors said it would never work - that he was trouble, that our morals were different and while he was a nice guy, our lives and futures wouldn't accommodate each other. If only I had taken heed to those insights. I would not have been so blinded to the things that happened to me.

When it began, life was good. We had so many plans and wanted to build our futures together. We shared so many of the same passions. I was completely vulnerable. In my immature mind we were one. I had been taught all my life in church that a husband and wife were one body, one flesh. My mistake was not truly realizing that, although he had taken my virginity and we had plans to get married after college, I was not his wife, and he was not my husband. He would often argue that a piece of paper wouldn't make our feelings any stronger; that he loved me the same and more every day that passed.

He was wrong.

Thankfully it was that frame of thinking, that saved me. I believed that marriage was God sanctioned, and that it was more than just a piece of paper. I must admit, at times I only wanted to be married to him because I felt it would tie us together and force us to work through our differences. This was a faulty way of thinking, as it would've only led to divorce, or perhaps my death. We were extremely flawed in our thinking and in all our ways. The things I imagined would make us better, made us worse.

In a sense I attempted to make a husband out of him, before God had even made him a man. Stepping completely out of order, I chased him - both physically and spiritually - but spiritually he was always unavailable. Rather than being the light, I led him in the wrong direction and in many ways weakened his ability to find God. I was a hypocrite; and while the excuse, "I'm not perfect" is not good enough, it was all I could offer.

I still remember the day our parents moved us into college. We were so excited to be there, but I cried as they pulled away from our dorm, leaving us at the university. Little did I know those tears foreshadowed the sorrow and regret I would feel. It took a sexually transmitted infection, a possible miscarriage, two breakups, three years, a bout with depression and, finally, him trying to sleep with my friend for me to figure out that he was bad for my life.

I would've done anything for him - no amount of money or success would have taken me away. He dropped out after our freshmen year, but I stayed with him, even with his paranoia about my life on campus. Sadly, I couldn't see that he didn't have those same feelings towards me. He was selfish and didn't care about anyone but himself. I felt like

I was dying. I couldn't take any more mistakes or apologies. Loving him had taken a toll on my mind, spirit, and body. I was physically and mentally drained, tired of praying for and about him. I wasn't what he wanted or needed. He needed someone to follow him blindly, straight into hell. I wasn't willing to do that, yet, still, he made my life feel like hell.

After everything we had been through my heart was crushed. I won't sit here and play the victim; we both had our faults. I was extremely wrong for showing him the things I did. I knew that fornication was wrong, and I should've held to my standards rather than conforming to social norms. I claimed to be a Christian yet did not understand what that fully meant. Beyond not upholding Christian behaviors, I was also ill-equipped to disciple him. I couldn't explain my reasons for believing in God to him the way he would have preferred. I wasn't able to argue science, nor did I have the desire to coexist. What I did know was that I loved God and that I loved Darrin.

The question then became, "How could I contain both?" I would eventually love one and despise the other. I was not in the business of leaving God, so the only choice was to walk away from the relationship. While it wasn't easy, I began to understand why this decision was vital to my growth; not only as a Christian, but as a woman.

My dependency on his approval was unhealthy. It was to the point to where I altered my life to fit the things, he felt were suitable. My actions and decisions were based on what our future would be like together, rather than finding my own individuality, or where God desired to lead me. I began to take on his characteristics. He believed that marriage was just a piece of paper, and therefore useless. In an effort to please him, I aligned my life with his; strongly considering and eventually embracing these views. Foolishly I went back on the decisions I had made to better my life. Time after time I allowed him back into my life, only to humiliate me.

Our last breakup was the first time I felt what it's like when God forcefully removes someone from your life. I felt like I was experiencing a plague. As I recall the scene, I think about the prophet Moses. He was to the point of death because of his disobedience to God's commandment to circumcise his son and the relief that came after his wife completed the task. Everywhere I turned there was trouble. I had gotten into a car accident and lost my car, I was physically sick and emotionally and spiritually drained. At one point I could not even get out of bed. I was unable to eat, walk, and I was struggling to breathe. I would go to different doctors, only for them to not be able to find out what was wrong with me. I would have allergic reactions to the medications they prescribed.

One day, about one week into this ordeal, I had a friend from high school, that I had not heard from in years, reach out to me. I began to share with her that I had been sick. She told me that God had given her Romans 1:18-32 concerning me.

As I begin to look up the scripture, I noticed it was one I was all too familiar with. It spoke of God's wrath against humanity's sin, specifically idolatry, sexual immorality and lust. It told of how God gave them over to a reprobate or corrupt mind. I knew then that I could no longer have any connection or relationship with him. I immediately texted him and let him know that we could no longer be together, be friends or communicate. This would be our very last break-up.

Within a day or so I was well enough to go back to school. He'd soon come to the campus to visit soon, and even without my presence being known, I'd learn of his true character once again as he would make out and attempt to sleep with a mutual friend.

I was thankful that the relationship ended. He was once someone who I felt I could not breathe without. Now, as I inhale and exhale, I realize it was a very immature relationship. I could not imagine my life going on without that relationship at the time. I thought he would always hold a place in my heart. I am embarrassed that it took so much pain for me to realize that he was not worth the energy I put into him. I used to wonder whether he was a demon or giant created specifically to attack my life, with hopes of destroying me.

These beliefs only increased as I began to experience a more demonic side of him that allowed him to burn bibles, and even actively advocate against Christianity. He had an ability to influence those around him to give up their beliefs, and social media tools such as Facebook and Twitter helped him reach a larger audience.

I eventually realized how seriously he took his personal mission of denouncing and disproving Christianity. I can still remember an ordeal that I was able to feel the presence of a spirit he was acting in. Prior to our final breakup, our reason for reconnecting was that he had asked me to help him understand God. He wrote me a letter, hoping that after several months of being apart we could reconnect because he was now willing to be more open to God. Foolishly, I returned and began to spend time with him; rarely, if ever, studying the bible because, just as before, it always led to arguments.

While sleeping at his house one day I could feel a demonic force over me, paralyzing me. I couldn't do anything but pray. I remember calling on the name of Jesus several times and feeling it break from over me. Sadly, I still wouldn't wash my hands of the situation. It took him making out with and attempting to sleep with my friend before I would leave him alone. I would realize that this was a cycle that would eventually kill me. First with chlamydia, then with exposure to HPV, depression, thoughts of suicide, and I could only imagine what would follow. To make matters worse, this was during a time where I was actively trying to get pregnant, in hopes of keeping him around.

The one thing I learned was that I should never be in a relationship with someone who didn't share the same spiritual values as me. To many this may sound closed-minded; I'm sure there are atheists all over the world who will shun me, calling me a dogmatic bible thumper. I am then led to argue that a house divided against itself cannot stand. How can two people walk together unless they agree upon the direction in which they walk? This opens the door for spiritual confusion in the home and creates an unstable platform to raise families and build lives. Followers of Christ, most of whom will at one point in their life marry, must realize the danger of being unequally yoked with non-believers.

As believers and followers of Christ we must walk in the spirit. Although this is a constant battle, our goal should be to progressively embody the attributes of Christ. Our goal in building families should always be that they are formed as God has declared that they should be, with the husband leading the household spiritually. In contrast to our beliefs, non-believers can only walk in the flesh. They are unable to soundly hear God's voice and lead Christian families, because they have chosen not to seek God's direction and abide in his will. This makes it impossible to fully trust your mate, because you have been stripped of the moral standard of how both your family and personal affairs should be kept. How can I be led by a man I feel I cannot trust?

The issue of being unequally yoked goes far beyond the cause of not being able to trust your potential spouse at the appointed time of marriage; however, other questions arise when you can't account for or appreciate the person they will become in the future. This is a concept that I wouldn't understand until later in life. At the age of eighteen, I couldn't quite grasp that God's Spirit truly did not hold the power over this tainted relationship - and neither did I. God was not present in that relationship, because he had not been invited in.

Family members bombarded me with questions about Darrin at an event a few years later, as I approached the end of my college years. They wanted to know whether we were still involved. Over the next couple of years numerous friends and family members enquired of his whereabouts, requesting that I stay far away from him, because our lifestyles and paths were completely different. I praise God for his grace and his mercy in bringing me out of that relationship. I never cared to confirm his struggles, or what route his life took after our relationship ended. In my eyes it was not my business, nor was it my concern. I was just in deep awe and greatly appreciative that God had many years before brought me out and covered my life.

Chapter Four:
Turn Down for What?

"Fire up that loud
Another round of shots
Shots, shots, shots, shots, shot, sh...

Turn down for what?"

-DJ Snake & Lil Jon

Chapter Four: Turn Down for What?

Turn down for what? Well, for starters, turn down because it's not who you were called to be. It's so easy to get distracted and detour away from your goals, dreams and deeply imbedded desire to do God's will. For many years during college, I devoted my time and life to seeking God. While I wasn't perfect, my desire was to be in his will, so much so that I broke up with my high school sweetheart because he decided to become an atheist. I decided that I wanted to live for God, and I was on a mission to hear his voice. When the leaders of the church said to seek his face, I took that very literally.

Sitting in my on-campus college apartment, staring at the white walls, waiting to hear the voice of God, and to once again speak in my heavenly language, I recommitted myself to God, asking him to help me rebuild my life. So much had transpired in such little time. At the age of 22, I was entering my senior year of college and life was well again; well, for the most part. It had been almost a year and a half since breaking up with Darrin, and I had cleaned not only my house, but my life, eliminating anything that I thought would distract me from God's plan. At this point I had been sitting in my apartment for months, not engaging in the party lifestyle. My focus was solely on school, God and working out to lose weight.

I prayed restlessly to God, but the issues I faced with waiting on him were not as severe as the challenges I was about to walk into, as I left his will because of frustration. I wanted God, but I wanted him immediately. What I didn't realize until much later is that he was actively present and creating in me a better life already, but because I didn't audibly hear his voice or receive direction, I moved out and did my own thing in rebellion. I had decided I was going to enjoy the last year and a half of college.

Each day I laid on my apartment floor; music playing, studying and crying out to God. For months I looked at four white walls and separated myself from everything to be with God. I had made a list of areas in my life that I needed and wanted God to move in. Months passed and I still couldn't audibly hear the voice of God.

"Why could everyone else hear him?" I thought. "Why is it so hard for me?," I thought.

And after months of trying, I gave up; even to the point that I stopped meeting my prayer and study times, out of frustration and perhaps disappointment. I figured it just wasn't my time. The inner me, the flesh, reasoned that I was young and perhaps I should just enjoy myself my last year of college. I decided it was time for me to TURN UP!

Turn Up! It was one of the most popular phrases during that time, a greeting used to let someone know It was time to party or drink. I would periodically attend campus or house parties my first two years of college, mostly the events hosted by on-campus organizations. I'd drink lightly, occasionally with my best friend in celebration of a birthday or the end of the semester, but never heavily. All that would change, as I decided that senior year would be my time, that I'd live my life.

I started off feeling convicted by the Holy Spirit to not give into that lifestyle, but after a while it became easier to push past my feelings of not belonging and just enjoy the parties, no matter how crazy I felt or looked. Truth be told, I stuck out like a sore thumb. I couldn't dance, I struggled to dress myself and I would always need assistance from friends to try to fit in with the crowd. I went out and drank heavily every night Sunday through Saturday, often staying up from sunrise to sunrise.

I took shots of tequila and screamed "YOLO!" (an acronym standing for you only live once) as often as possible and attended my 8 a.m. classes still intoxicated from partying just hours before. I began to smoke marijuana and do numerous other things I wasn't supposed to do such as use profanity, facilitate underage drinking and drive under the influence of alcohol. I viewed it as being able to live free and make mistakes. I thought it didn't matter because I had time. All this would end soon, and I'd be going back home to be the preacher's kid. It wouldn't be until an entire year later that I would see the consequences of my actions. It would be only by God's grace that I would come out with both my degree and sanity. It was an easy introduction to partying, drugs, and alcohol, but soon I'd engage in another relationship, outside of God's will once again, and it would become a catalyst of turmoil that would impact every area of my life.

It's not easy to describe the relationship or lack thereof. Millennials sometimes use the term situationship to describe people who they've never officially been in a relationship with, but the feelings they shared were deep enough to cause uncertainty between the two parties. Well, that was us, John and I were unofficially official. We shared that lets eat, lets drink, that can't wait to see you, go hang out, have sex, catch feelings for one another and figure out what to do with them later type of love. If there is nothing else that I can say about him, it's that he was sincere at best - at times to my detriment.

He and I never had any problems with each other as far as physically fighting, he was always a gentleman. Spiritually he never claimed to be a disciple of Christ, but I never once heard about him burning a bible. I would occasionally catch him in the library singing gospel songs, so I figured I was already ahead of the last relationship. Honestly, I was afraid to ask him about his beliefs. I really didn't have the strength, ability or desire to battle with God, yet again. I figured ignoring the question would be best. Years later I'd be surprised to know that he was someone that God would use to keep me from myself, to pull me out of a very dark space. Regardless of what his beliefs were, he believed in who I was destined to become.

When our situationship first began, I wasn't very known on campus, at least not on the party scene. When people heard my name, they thought about someone who carried herself in a respectable manner. I was known for being active on campus, for all the right reasons such as leading campus organizations or organizing events, but that would soon drastically change. The only college legacy I left behind was that of a groupie for a Black Greek fraternity. He was only the second man I had ever been intimate with. By the time people found out about it, we had been seeing each other on a long-term basis, but none of this mattered. It was just easier for people to label me a whore, especially when he never spoke up to confirm or deny it. Perhaps he was trying to please everyone or be non-confrontational, but either way it left me out in the cold, with the world laughing and pointing fingers.

The truth is, without any official titles, or commitment, women and men, friends and foes alike, felt comfortable enough to disrespect me. I was a joke, because I took him seriously, and he did exactly what he wanted to do. There's a saying that goes, "What's understood doesn't have to be explained." It's one of the most asinine ideals that I've ever embraced, and this way of thinking ultimately attributed to much of my humiliation.

In actuality, there is a great need for what is understood to be explained, so that you have a verbal standard of what the goals and rules are. We had no roadmap or timeline of where we were going, or what we were doing, thus it placed me in the same boat as every other girl he was sleeping with. Truth is, because we had no timeline, no goals, and no commitment, I was just like those other girls. Yes, he liked me, enough to sleep with me and perhaps even be my friend, but he had no intention of ever committing to me.

He did not plan a present or future with me, simply because he did not desire to, although I wouldn't realize that until many years later. In the moment, I foolishly settled for being a favorite, if I was even that. The first time I told him I loved him, he didn't respond. I don't believe people should reciprocate verbal responses to feelings if they don't truly feel that way, but that should have at least been a red flag or signal of his unavailability.

It was easy for other women out of jealousy, or even just out of spite to treat me like a groupie or a joke. There was no conflict within their spirits in their attempts to humiliate and demean my reputation by nominating and electing me to receive the campus groupie award. After all we were never official, and regardless of how much I thought we liked each other, it's quite possible he had the same scenario being played out with multiple young women.

Ultimately, I believe I was targeted because the scenario was different from what people expected of us. People began to see a different side of him and of me. As someone who had always been known for his promiscuity, the idea of him committing to someone was unbelievable. It was easy for them to body-check or bump me on campus, toss drinks on me, or even key my sister's car; with no regard for my humanity. In no way do I accept or condone their behavior, bullying is never acceptable, but in reflection I realize how my actions made me a target.

How could I hold them to a moral standard, that I no longer met? How could they respect me, if I didn't demand he respect me or if I didn't respect myself? Foolishly I accepted being in the gray area, this in-between space where each party could do as they pleased. On top of that, I had chosen to entangle myself yet again in a situation and with a person God didn't intend me to be involved with. It would take getting in a heap of legal trouble before I'd realize just how far from God I had drifted.

The irony was that although I was labeled as the groupie, he was often the one pouring out his feelings for me to our mutual friends, and even my family members. I can recall numerous incidents at the local bars on campus, or even social gatherings, where he would become emotional concerning our relationship. He'd often pull friends to the side questioning whether or not I truly wanted to be with him. Even with our lack of commitment, there were still milestones that we experienced that are parallel to a traditional relationship, such as meeting parents or siblings. From the very first day he met my sisters, he embraced them as his own and their relationships remained even after the demise of ours.

May 27, 2013.

It's a date I'll never forget. I was involved in two physical altercations within 15 minutes of each other. I was drinking at an on-campus apartment when Sidney, a girl who had been harassing me for the past year, showed up. I decided to leave the gathering, but I couldn't stop myself from making some comments on the way out the door. The comments escalated into us fighting in the parking lot - in front of a crowd of 15 or so.

A big part of the reason Sidney didn't like me was that her best friend, Cassidy, used to sleep with John. Cassidy lived close to where the fight took place and got wind of it, so when my best friend Nicole and I fled the scene in her car, Sidney and Cassidy followed behind us. They blocked our car in the driveway of a house. We got out to fight again. This time I fought Cassidy, and the police had to tase me off her. All four of us were arrested.

To add insult to injury, I was denied a personal protection order by the court and I had to fight a misdemeanor charge of disorderly conduct. The taser and the two hours in jail were the lighter of the afflictions in comparison to the money, time and energy wasted going to court and paying fines. The issues with these girls would go on for years, even after graduating from college. The only thing we had in common was that we had slept with John.

In addition to court, that summer progressively got worse, and my legal troubles didn't end there. By the time August hit, I was in a whirlpool of fire that only God could save me from. My heart and desire to be a good friend, often got me in trouble. I naively rented audio equipment for one of his frat brothers that I was close to, and the equipment was stolen from a party. On top of my court charges, I was now responsible for $2000.00 worth of missing equipment. I'd be responsible to repay for the equipment, minus $200 that was given to me. I was completely outdone, and over college, court and my situationships. I didn't think I could take anymore, yet still more came.

My turmoil hit its climax a week later. My doctor called and told me he found abnormal cell changes on my cervix. He said he would need to monitor me over the next two years to ensure they weren't cancerous. I spent the next two weeks buried under blankets in my best friends' apartment, feeling as though I was damaged goods. There are no limits to the things that ran through my mind. I questioned whether any man would want to be with me, and if I would ever be able to have children. I spent time reflecting on my sexual partners, and finally praying that out of the hundreds of strands of HPV, that it wasn't the wart-producing virus. I would be blessed to never experience genital warts or have to take any medication, but nothing compared to the pain of having this linger over me for the next two years, let alone the rest of my life, because of unwise decisions I made to leave God's ark of safety.

This emotional, on-again, off-again cycle of connection went on for years with John, even during other relationships. We would often go years or months without speaking or engaging and then suddenly pick up where we left off, like nothing ever ended or came between us. At one point I had been celibate for over two years, and within one homecoming weekend, I was back consistently involved with him, even with us living hundreds of miles apart. We lived in two different cities with three hundred miles between us and consistently both parties would drive multiple times in any given month to visit one another. The soul ties ran deep between the two of us. It's so important to set boundaries with who you're connected to. Spiritual, emotional and sexual ties have the ability to interrupt and destroy progress. These are strongholds that have to be broken by God, and then you must still place boundaries on your interaction. Each time he'd resurface, I'd break my vow of celibacy.

So sure, he and I had no problem with physical fighting. He wasn't a bible burning atheist, and overall, he was a relatively decent person; but the issues I faced were far more severe because my decision to backslide and my lust for him stole something much more meaningful - my self-worth. Prior to my turn-up phase, God had been replenishing what was damaged in my last relationship. He had been building self-imagery within me and coached me to see myself the way that he saw me, teaching me, what it really meant to be created in his image. I foolishly exchanged the way God saw me to become a clone of who everyone else was pretending to be.

I misunderstood God being silent, for God being inactive. Although I could not hear him, I was actively learning about him and myself. He was working, even though I could not see what he was doing. In my semester of solitude, I earned some of the best grades I've ever received in college, I set and accomplished weight-loss goals, and I learned about God's word. I exchanged these things for the ability to party and barely graduated from college.

I had lost myself on so many different levels. My morals, values, ideals, goals and dreams were shattered. It would take years to repair and move back in the direction of meeting my academic goals. It would take me losing everything, self-image included, before I would run back to God crying, and begging him to fix my life. With my mind confused and my heart hurting. I soon began to spend time with God. Slowly, he revealed the changes that had occurred in me. I no longer possessed the strength that I once had, the joy and knowledge of his word, but God was ready to restore

Chapter Five: Pinky Promise: Mission Failed

"There hath no temptation taken you but such as is common to man: but God is faithful, who will not suffer you to be tempted above that ye are able; but will with the temptation also make a way to escape, that ye may be able to bear it."

1 Corinthians 10:13 King James Version (KJV)

Chapter Five: Pinky Promise: Mission Failed

In August of 2013 I packed up a U-haul of my belongings, which included legal turmoil and a broken heart, and I moved back in with my mom and dad in Detroit. Only this time it wasn't just us, I'd come home to a plethora of responsibilities, both financial and otherwise. My parents had given up their house to start a transitional center for young women aging out of foster care. I came home as the big sister to fifteen girls, and new sisters were being added weekly. My (blood) sister and I took the basement of the 21-bedroom facility and turned it into our apartment, a mini hiatus from all the depressing factors that existed around us. With no job, no money, and most of my friends still at school, the only thing familiar to me was the accessibility to alcohol. So that's exactly what I did, I drank. I remember many days when my sister and I would sit on the basement floor looking around us, wondering how we got to this point and crying that we wanted our lives back. In between us would be a gallon of 1800 Silver Tequila, with no chasers. We'd sit and drink, remembering the days not too far behind us, when we were in the midst of friends on campus enjoying the drinks that now helped drown us in our sadness of these times ending.

As time went on, there became a heaviness of the growing responsibilities that I had. I couldn't find a job anywhere, at least not one that paid enough for me to survive outside of daily living. I could only afford the gas to get there and a few groceries. I was angry that I had went and paid for a college degree that I wasn't able to put to good use. To say that I was in debt was an understatement. Bills kept coming in - university debt, student loans, credit cards, phone bills - not to mention travel fees and court fines. Legal issues continued to arise, as the audio company filed papers to sue me after the theft of the rented speakers. To make matters worse, I soon learned that I had failed my last class, which meant I would have to pay out of pocket to retake the class. The class wasn't offered again until the next fall, which meant I had to wait before I could officially receive my degree. I felt consumed with everything, and I remember it being hard to breathe without tears. It became harder to pull myself out of the bed, and even harder to separate me from the bottles of alcohol. Life hit me hard. We had just celebrated my college graduation months prior, yet, by the time October hit, I felt like a huge failure. There was nothing I wanted more than a chance to redo the last year and a half of my life. I realized just how drastically my grades, reputation and mindset had changed.

On top of everything, as any parents would, mine began to put pressure on me about getting back into church and doing the work they said I was called to do. I wasn't too sure about being called to do anything anymore. Yes, I absolutely loved God, but work in the ministry, as a leader? After all I'd just done and was currently doing?

The one thing I did know was to not play with God. I knew, or at least I thought that when I stepped into whatever he desired for me, I'd need to come correct. I realize this is where many people make the mistake of waiting to get their life together before coming back to Christ. The idea of using your own strength to get your life back seems tempting, but it is also counterproductive to Christ. We can never fix and mold our lives like God can, at least not to his standards. I don't have the story of, using my own talents and strengths to pull myself out, in fact I didn't go back because of me, although I definitely knew I was in need of salvation. Truth be told, I could have just wasted my life away in that basement, crying, sleeping, and drinking; but upstairs were young girls who desired an older sister, and each of them helped pull me out.

I had always been an older sister, with four younger birth siblings. Responsibility was not a stranger to me. Living in a building and sharing a community bathroom with two dozen girls, however, was new. I had to share my parents, I had to cook meals, give advice, help with schoolwork, and if that wasn't enough, they were now coming to me about spiritual matters. Many of them were broken and were dealing with far worse issues at much younger ages. They were in desperate need of God to mend their broken pieces. Even if I was in a low place, I didn't have any room for a pity party - literally. There was always someone knocking on the door, peeking their heads in and smiling around the corner. There was always a new girl, each with a story more heartbreaking than the last.

I caught on to the vision that God had given my parents. I began to see them set free by the Holy Spirit and unknowingly began to build relationships with them. My mother had also lectured me on how I was a leader, whether I wanted to be one or not, and so I thought the least I could do was be a vessel for God, if he still desired to use what was left inside of me. The least I could do was to help teach someone else, even if it wasn't spiritual, but with the educational necessities and life skills. So, I put the liquor bottle down, took a vow of celibacy, and hit the ground running. Within days we started having events in the house, hosting youth days at church, and doing give backs in the community. We hosted bible studies every morning at 6 a.m., where I taught on different topics that impact young women.

Things begin to progress with the youth and the ministry continued to advance. My mom had the reputation of being able to build a rapport and glean respect from some of the ladies that were listed as high-risk or as having some of the worst attitudes within the foster care system. We began to average about 20-24 girls in the home. During one of our dinner events we received a new girl and, little did I know, she would become one of my best friends. She inspired me to desire more out of life. She would help me believe in myself and in what God desired to do for me again. Into the dining room she walked, with her small stature, and toned muscular arms carrying a small car seat with a baby whose legs were spilling over the ends.

Autumn was quiet at first and gave the impression that she had no desire to be here. She spoke no words to anyone else, but soon after our session ended she'd stay behind and ask me what my name was and I'd respond that she could call me by my nickname, "Kyda", and she would crack a smile, showing her braces and beautiful high cheekbones, and respond, "Ok, you gon' be my sister." She asked whether she could play in my hair and do my eyebrows. I was reluctant at first, but in an effort to build a relationship with her, I said yes. Well, let's just say she SLAYED my hair, my eyebrows and my spirit. We stayed up for hours talking about life. She wanted to know everything about me, about my life, about my future, my heartache and she encouraged me beyond what I can measure.

Autumn shared her story with me, how she had experienced the death of her daughters' father less than a year prior, at the age of sixteen. She told me of her rape and molestation experiences, causing us to cry together over the physical abuse she had endured. We laughed at our foolish mistakes, and we cheered as her daughter took her first steps. I candidly spoke with her as my friend, as my sister, and she saved me. She constantly spoke into my life that I was good enough, and that God was going to change my life around.

Together we began to move. We made plans to meet every day in the pink conference room on the computers to work on our futures. She wanted to own a boutique and I wanted to start a nonprofit. We'd get up every day and get dressed, faces full of makeup, only to go to the conference room and work on our futures. It wouldn't be too long before she had convinced me to move out of the basement and into a bedroom across from hers. Although I was moving, and asking God for my way out, it wasn't long before the pink conference room, lined with all white walls became my place of solitude. Again, I was waiting on God.

I had begun to feel much better. Still, I would sit in the pink room alone for hours, trying to figure out what had gone wrong with my life and how could I get it back on track. It seemed so fast that life had been turned upside down. One of my favorite things to do was search Google to see if people had blogged, or chatted about situations similar to the ones I had found myself in. I'd soon come to realize - there wasn't a replica. I would never find someone with my upbringing, with my pain and stories. It didn't exist, and even if similar stories did - I'd always find a way to diminish their stories because I viewed them through the paradigm of my own pain.

I would eventually run into ministers like Sara Jakes Roberts and Heather Lindsey. Heather Lindsey's story and testimony resounded in my mind, and I learned more about her blog and organization, Pinky Promise. One post that stands out to me was entitled "Sooo, how was your first kiss on your wedding day?! Was it worth the wait?!" In it she discussed her reason, challenges and triumph in courtship with her husband. Most importantly, she shared a story of holiness, and God's desire for us to be set apart, not to conform to the world's standard of dating. She challenged young women to uphold God's standard, by sharing how she and her husband waited until their wedding day to share their first kiss. Aww! How beautiful, right? Well, not to someone with a pessimistic mindset.

I had such a toxic way of thinking. I felt as though something like that could never happen for me, "She doesn't have my history," I said to myself. "No man will ever wait for me." I questioned what a courtship would even look like. "How would someone go months or even years without having sex, or even kissing for that matter?" I thought, "Even if it happened for her, I'm damaged goods."

I had been taught to reason using the logic of the rule of thumb, and that you are rarely, if ever, the exception to the rule. In my carnal mind, I looked at the natural attributes that made us different. She was beautiful - light complexion, nice, thin figure, ;pshe also went to a Big Ten school and had a very good job. I thought because of these things, the access she had to men had put her in a better position. I had listened to her say that it was all Godly divine and orchestrated, but I could not bridge the distance between us. I didn't see that the one connection that she and I shared alike- was the love of our father, Jesus Christ. It was to my own detriment that I didn't understand his love and walk in its possibilities sooner.

I would watch her blogs, because they gave me hope. The truth is, they fed my spirit-man. The more I watched, the more I talked to God about my problems. I remember asking God whether this was even possible for me, and if so, could I have it? I so desperately wanted to get love right. I wanted a Godly divine and orchestrated love story. I wanted that, "Let's wait until marriage, wake up to each other in love, pray together, fast together, have babies and accomplish God's plan for our lives type of love."

But it just seemed so unattainable.

Nonetheless, I took Heather Lindsey up on her challenge. The part of the plan that I did not do so well at was eliminating distraction and severing old ties. I'd practice celibacy for over two years. I'd actively pursue holiness; I'd get back into to church and even begin working in the ministry. I'd eliminate secular music, dating, partying, drinking, etc, but eventually, when the test circled back around, I'd fumble, allowing my appetite for men outside of God's will to distract me once again.

Chapter Six:
More Than I Could Chew

"Don't bite off more than you can chew because nobody looks attractive spitting it back out."

— Carroll Bryant

Chapter Six: More Than I Could Chew

It's strange the things people do for love. I once turned my world upside down for somebody because I thought that maybe I had found a love that might be true. I was coming off a hook up with John at Homecoming and bitterly disappointed with myself after. He was unavailable. He might not have had a girlfriend, but he wasn't ever going to be my boyfriend. It was never going to work out, yet I kept up the vicious cycle. I was disappointed in the whole situation, but mostly with myself.

Eric caught me at the perfect time to be destroyed. He walked into my world pretending to be a friend, but ultimately preyed on my insecurities and led me down a terrible path of humiliation and pain. As I struggled to rebuild my identity, something I always promised myself I would never lose, I found myself conflicted in a deep search for what I deserved and trying to reason with myself that better relationships were available to me. I battled with what I would stand for, and how much pain I would take in a relationship, all because I did not want to be alone.

He made love feel like an addictive drug. I would've done anything to get my fix of Eric - the high of being in love, continuously reading over our old love letters and imagining the words coming off his lips, as well as his touch. I wanted and needed my fix of him, even if it meant just for a moment; because that was all the time we had. I cherished that time - moments stolen from the woman he would soon make his wife. When she called, we would have an awkward silence, only to return to passion and laughter after. I looked forward to the nights I could steal him away, so that we could wake up next to one another in my bed. Inevitably he'd leave, though, and I'd go back to being lonely.

My decision to give my heart away went against my recent vow, to wait on God's direction to lead me to my mate. I had just completed a four-week bible study where we discussed the relationship of Mary and the Holy Trinity. Through this I taught that when God gave Mary the task of birthing our Savior, Jesus Christ, the person that she was connected to had to be trusted with her assignment as well. I had just taught to a small group that those we intimately surround ourselves with have to be on the same mental and spiritual wavelength as us concerning their walk. Yet within weeks I had failed the test attached to my own message, yet again. For the third time I fell head over heels for a man that didn't love the God I serve; the God that I have pledged to devote my life and work too. Each time it took away a piece of me that believed that love existed, and I had already lost two big ones. The truth of the matter was, I had always stated that I didn't want a husband that was a pastor, preacher or heavily involved in the church. To a certain extent I was pushing away the very people I probably should've been dating, yet there he was.

Our connection seemed almost magnetic from the very beginning. It started with a smile, then a prolonged handshake during our introduction in the staff lounge. It was as easy as breathing. Our conversations from the first "Hello" were filled with a calm peace that unclouded the clustery chaos of my mind. I felt comfortable exposing my deepest secrets without a doubt or question concerning his character, as if I had known him for years. To call him trustworthy might have been an understatement; because there was as a surreal aura surrounding him that I had never experienced before.

I was myself with him (at least at first); a hopeless romantic, corny, uncompromisingly stubborn, and impulsively passionate person, who later tries to make her actions rational, naturally guarded and naïve. He read me like a book, and although at the time I didn't understand it, I would soon realize that his nontraditional take on life and unorthodox spiritual lifestyle would hinder me in going further into my purpose; I'd come to realize that life with him wouldn't always be fairy tales, rainbows and sunshine.

He was unlike anyone I'd ever met before, and everything about him made me fearful. It was an all-too familiar experience for me; he was another who would soon join the list of that which was off limits. It seemed like I would only meet what I thought was his kind - men outside the will of God. One of the first questions he asked me was "What attracted me to him?" because he was "worldly," to which I responded, "Why do you consider yourself worldly?" I thought to myself, "Not again. Lord, why am I always drawn to atheists?" I had written him off to be something that was detrimental to me. The truth was, I didn't know how to approach a friendship or lack thereof. There was still a space inside of me that was worldly, and that is what attracted us. The more I avoided him, the more drawn to him I became. Eventually we created a bond and shared an experience that would help reshape and redefine the paradigm in which I viewed men in general.

I was afraid. Everything in my mind told me to run the opposite way every time I saw him coming down the halls or walk into the staff lounge. I had only been working at the school for a week when we had our first encounter. Although I truly wanted to know more about him and I felt comfortable with him, a part of me believed that what attracted us wasn't the light, or at least not the light as I understood it. I was attracted to the easiness of our conversations, the relaxed nature of our interaction. I didn't have to try or focus on cultivating anything because we had a natural bond.

He read me like a book, it was as if he had a gift. He approached me with salutations, and quickly begin to read what was going on in my life. He asked personal questions, questions about my troubles and where my headspace was currently. Being so accurate, I eventually shared with him my struggles. That week prior to starting work, I had broken my two years of celibacy by sleeping with John at Homecoming.

Eric responded by giving me his number, and saying to call him later after work, because he needed to make it back to class. I initially thought we'd have an older brother-younger sister or uncle-niece type of friendship. Sadly, that idea of a sibling-like friendship would change within the next few hours.

The first night we ever spoke over the phone, we prayed for one another, and I found myself asking God, "Lord, is this my husband?" I had never met anyone like him before, and I was so intrigued by the level of openness and intimacy in our conversations. I had never experienced anything like it before, it was mind-blowing. I soon began to cross items off my checklist: he was smart, funny and charismatic. I had completely decided to look past my other desires that he lacked. He wasn't tall, nor did he have nice teeth, but he did have a dapper meets hipster style that fit his personality.

My attraction to men with a bulky, athletic build also went out of the window, because I had learned that Eric transformed his body into what it was. He had recently lost weight, and that was a struggle for me that he understood. I stood 5 feet 5 inches tall, weighing in at 203 pounds. He agreed to be my personal trainer. That was his way into my world, the place where we connected.

It wasn't long before we were working out together, meeting for lunch daily and hanging outside of work. He began visiting my church, met my parents, and attended birthday parties and family events. Next, came writing love letters, gifts and merging personal lives. He was the first man that I allowed to know the real me; he encouraged me to be open about my fears, past, desires, goals and struggles; something I would soon come to regret.

Things moved rather quickly between us. About three weeks from our introduction, we began spending a lot of time together. A few weeks later he revealed that he was actually in a relationship. Still after that, I'd find out that they lived together. She FaceTimed him during one of our workout sessions, and I overheard him complaining about someone being needy and just not wanting to let go. It was then that he revealed that he had been in an on-again, off-again relationship with a young woman for the past five years. He went on to say that she provided an element of growth and stability that he lacked. He felt as if he was getting too old to keep starting over, and she was more financially stable and helping him to build wealth.

Upon finding out about their relationship, I expressed that wasn't okay with being a part of their situation, and he gave me the option of not having anything to do with him. That was something I took him up on, and a week went by without us communicating. He soon asked whether we could speak privately. We ended up talking in his truck after work one day, where he shared with me that they had just vacationed in Miami. He said that before the trip he purchased a ring and wanted to propose to her, but that things didn't feel right over the vacation. He added that the proposal didn't go as planned, because things felt off without me, and he withheld the ring. A few days later, he slipped a promise ring on my finger, saying he wanted to build a future with me. This ring had a gold band and peach stone, and although it was not my style, I cherished it because of the promise that was attached.

Over the next couple of weeks, he began to move out of their place and began moving his belongings into my new, one-bedroom apartment. He began staying over days at a time, and when he wasn't there, I was told that he was staying with his mother and daughter who lived in Flint, Michigan. I believed this to be true, because I had been to visit and met them both numerous times.

During this time, we also started to decorate my apartment so that it was conducive for both of our lifestyles. He was an artist, and we created a space for him to paint, as well as hang his work around the apartment. Rugs, tables, curtains, and preferred bedding soon followed. We even made plans to move into a loft in Midtown Detroit together. He changed everything: my schedule, my diet and even the atmosphere inside of my home. He brought a new plant or flower every time he returned to what had become our home. There were always tarot cards out, candles lit and sage burning. We often meditated before being sexually intimate.

In the movies, this type of setting is portrayed to be serene, sensual and deeply spiritual. That was partially what I felt, but only because I wanted to embrace Eric. I'd come to realize that there is a steep level of darkness attached to such depths of codependency. He took me to a realm that no one else had, and left me there alone, in the dark, in the cold, and without any protection - spirits and emotions battling to the point of chaos. He was able to control me, my body and mind yielded to whatever he desired. It took months of prayer, fasting and crying out to God to sever our soul ties, before I would receive deliverance.

A picture of the two of them during the holiday season, on Facebook, shattered the cage he had lured me into. I found out that he had still been seeing her and sleeping with the both of us, without protection.

It wasn't long before I noticed that I had bitten off more than I could chew. He formally shared with me later that he desired a polygamous relationship and lifestyle. This did not sit well with me, as I never desired to engage in this type of relationship.

He would continuously ask me, "Are you ready to meet her?"

My answer was always the same, "NO!"

My emotions spun out of control when he began to tell our male co-workers and his fraternity brothers that he was in a relationship with the both of us. I heard him explain that he was in two serious and committed relationships, and that everyone was fine with the terms. He would talk about the both of us together, and how he would give both of us children. He stated that he wanted me to give him a girl, because he saw a gifting inside of me for raising and teaching young women and that he wanted her to raise his boys, because she had grown up without a mother and lacked daintiness.

At times I wish that I would've had the opportunity to speak with her after my relationship with him ended. A part of me didn't know whether to believe him or not. Perhaps she was trapped in the same darkness that I experienced. I would never have the opportunity to meet her, but I would encounter another woman, who I can only pray made it out of his grips.

I could not recognize myself spiritually, physically, or in any other capacity. Everything about me had changed. I had not spent time with God in so long, I didn't even know how to pray for myself. While still in the relationship, I learned that he did not "subscribe to" or believe in Jesus, and he began sharing with me his spiritual walk and how he worshipped at Native American sweat lodges. After researching, I learned that a sweat lodge is a Native American tradition where people enter a dome-shaped hut to experience a sauna-like environment, while praying, singing, and chanting. Still clinging to my beliefs, but attempting to learn about his, I agreed to attend with him.

One afternoon soon after, I was asked to meet with him so that we could ride together to the sweat lodge. Upon arriving, I found out that another young woman would be joining us. Before I got into the vehicle, he made it a point to have a discussion with me about the need for kindness. He told me that she had never attended a sweat lodge and that she and I would share a very small space, that there may be times when we had to help one another because he would be on the other side of the hut with the men and would not be able to see or assist us.

I got into the car, and we drove silently after brief introductions. As we entered the hut, she and I walked together, both fearful of what we were about to experience. We crawled into the small space with about twenty other individuals both male and female. They began to sing and pray in both English and other languages. It seems like the ceremony went on for hours. They did several rounds of praying, passing water and singing.

Towards the end, she began to cough, and shared with me that she could not breathe. I encouraged her to press her faced close to the ground and I moved over to give her more room. Fearful of what was happening, I began to pray for her until it was over. As I prayed for her, I also prayed for myself. Now, more than ever, I wanted God to give me a way of escape. The ceremony would soon end, and, later that night, I drove her home. I never saw or heard about her again. All I knew was that I was losing myself, and very quickly I was becoming unrecognizable. Something had to change.

Before my own eyes, I had become them. I had become what I had once despised. I had become what I once called a weak spineless being, that validates a man in his mission to fail, one who allows a man to exist in mediocracy, rather than requiring him to be the man he promised to be. It wouldn't be long before I'd share with him that I didn't want to be a part of any of this anymore.

About two weeks later he asked me to get dressed up and meet him at his father's lounge. He asked me to give him a chance to make things right. Foolishly, I agreed. When I arrived, rather than going inside - he stopped me as I prepared to exit my car. He went on to say, "This isn't somewhere you want to be." He shared that it was more of a celebration for the two of them, and he thought it was best if I stayed outside.

I got back into my car, and I drove down 8 Mile at night in Detroit, in the middle of winter, with burning eyes and tears streaming down my face. I screamed at God because I couldn't understand why the man, I thought loved me was about to marry another woman; and how he could invite me to their engagement party. I sat in the car, hyperventilating and crying as the reality sat in that he had decided to propose to his long-term girlfriend. He had invited our co-workers and their families to his father's jazz lounge, and, in an effort to humiliate me and break down my self-esteem even more, he invited me.

The man I that had been praying for, my "Mr. Right," wasn't for me. I selfishly wanted for him to be mine so badly. I was tired of waiting. It had been two-and-a-half years since my last situationship, and I was ready. I was ready for love, I knew God. I was active in ministry, although I was struggling spiritually. I thought I was building my life, but I allowed someone to come in and shift my home into chaos. I still reasoned that I had everything someone might say a woman needs to experience or acquire before she is married. I wasn't financially dependent upon anyone, yet still I received the "L".

Nothing could help me understand why I kept taking a "loss" on good men, with good jobs and bright futures. This time it was even more of an insult because I managed to fall for someone who wasn't an atheist or agnostic, he had at least some modicum of beliefs. I thought for sure that God would have my back on this one. My sisters and I would always joke and say that "God would be looking out for us," as we dated with the intention of being married. But, the truth is, I didn't believe it. It was especially hard on that day because I could feel the fire of tears and the knots in my throat as a tried to stomach the truth of what was happening.

In efforts to find my way through this, I ran to the one person who I knew I loved more than him, another unbreakable soul tie, I ran back to John. He was the one person that I consistently went back to over the years. If nothing else, he had shown to be my friend, and I shared the most intimate and secret things concerning this experience with darkness. And, as I knew he would, he helped pull me out.

He told me I wasn't the kind of woman to be a side piece or baby momma, he told me that I desired to be loved. He told me that I was a wife, and although he wasn't in a place to love me the way I deserved, that he would never let me be with someone who didn't appreciate me the way I deserved to be. I shared with him the mental games being played, and the manipulation that had occurred. I cried as I told him of the incident inside the car, when I had been "playfully" slapped and bled profusely from my mouth. He held me and listened, not because of sex or because he had something to gain, but with compassion, the non-committer helped save me from myself.

Chapter Seven: Fearful Standards

"There was a time when our desire for each other would have landed us in an asylum or prison, had it not been sanctioned by mutual assent. True or false."

— Lawrence Krauser, Lemon

Chapter Seven: Fearful Standards

Approximately one month after my breakup, our breakup, I received a direct message from Eric on Instagram. I hesitated to open the message because I was unsure of its content. I had already been slightly fearful because, even though he had left the school months prior, he would continuously pop up and leave notes on my car, bring flowers into the office and email, call and text me. I figured, if I ignored him, he would eventually get the picture and go away. This turned out to be untrue, in fact, he would soon begin to send me images via text message and social media of dead mermaids. He knew that mermaids are my spirit animal, I've always loved them. There were mermaids all around my apartment, as well as art, plants and exotic flowers that he had given me.

Weeks after the breakup, my best friend pointed out, how strange it was that he showed up to every event we said we were attending on Facebook. Even after he had been blocked on the social network, I soon realized that he had created a duplicate profile and was still able to view my account. He would show up to my family events, as if we were still in communication, and ask to see me. Eventually I agreed to meet him at a Burger King during the day. During this setting I made it very clear that I did not want to be with him, that I was still dealing with my old college fling and had intentions on seeing whether John and I could work things out. I told him that he and I would no longer be able to communicate, but that I wished him the best. So, imagine my surprise when the email, notes and calls kept coming.

Reluctantly, I opened the direct message, only to find a screenshot of nude pictures I had sent him months before. Listed below the pictures where multiple hashtags which included #ExposingH*es, #Exposed, #KiaraAnniceHunter, #KYDA and #Nudes, among others. I was completely distraught. Despite the rumors from college, I had always prided myself on retaining a level of modesty with sexual partners. I had never slept around; in fact, I could count the number of men I'd slept with on one hand and still have fingers to spare. So, the idea that my body had been exposed to the world via social media caused me to fall apart. Suddenly, my world shook, I was fearful of everything around me. I had to question whether the artwork I was being sent of dead mermaid were threats against my life. My eyes were open, and I began to notice random occurrences, like cars of a similar color, make, and model to his being parked outside my apartment complex and job. I had an eerie feeling that I was being watched, with no way to prove whether it was him or not. I had learned from past experiences in college that restraining orders were not easy to get, so I began to document everything that was happening.

One morning in June, I walked outside to a poisonous plant wrapped around the banister of my apartment. I reported the incident, and by the time I got home from work, the plant had been removed by maintenance. My anxiety got so bad that within the next few weeks I changed my car, quit my job and moved back home with my parents. Sadly, these changes wouldn't be enough to make the occurrences stop. He was hired by the same company as my best friend, and attempted to converse with her, asking her to convey messages to me. Every year since then, he has called or reach out to me via email - with no response.

The thought of someone stalking me instantly filled me with fear. For years I watched my back, always on guard for things that could be thought of as a threat. I was careful of what information I put on social media, and who I allowed into my personal space. One of the things that this experience forced me to do was to set better standards for myself.

I decided that men would no longer be allowed inside my home. Many women might feel that's extreme, but after inviting someone into my space and having them violate me, I deemed this as a necessary precaution. My home is my comfort zone, it's where I am protected. I decided that this could only be broken after I was in an official relationship, when we had discussed intentional dating and courtship, after we had a clear understanding and conversation about not having premarital sex, and after my intentions contract has been signed (Yes! I was not playing, lol). I was exhausted and completely over dating aimlessly. I was tired of having my heart broken, body mistreated and spirit under attack. Every time I allow someone into my personal space, my home, it was defiled.

At this point I had lost two apartments due to my own sin. I wasn't comfortable or protected. I was fearful and, most importantly, I lost myself by allowing people, and whatever spirits had attached to them, to enter my temples, both my home and body. At a very young age I made the conscious decision to dedicate my body to God, giving it to use for his purpose, because I believe that he died and rose again for my sins. Yet, somehow, my biggest issue was sexual immorality. I continuously allowed the place where God dwells, where the holy spirit lives, and the place that would someday serve as a dwelling place for my husband, and children, to be defiled. I had made up my mind that this would never happen to me again. I was over casual dating.

My second standard was to be second only to God. Why? Because I deserved to be a priority only behind God. John was right, I wasn't created to do the main chick, side chick, polygamist, secret relationships thing, or to date men who didn't love my God. If I wanted to be with someone, it needed to be God ordained. I realized my standards had to align with my expectations.

My third standard was to never go back to a relationship that I had left, which meant that my half-a-decade-long, college situationship turned friendship with John had to go as well. I told myself that there were reasons why it ended, and to keep those reasons in the forefront of my mind. I urged myself to hold true to those reasons and allow myself time to heal and grow. I had ended every relationship, and ceased all communication, and I remember feeling sorrow and as if a state of depression was lingering.

I remember walking into the office at work and receiving counsel from my work mom. She was a woman of wisdom, and she had experienced life in many forms. She looked at me and told me to leave the building and take a personal day. She poured into me spiritually, giving me what is possibly the best advice I've ever received - to take time to feel the emotions that were leaving me. She shared that grief comes in many forms, and it was okay to feel these pressures and experience this hurt, if I didn't let it paralyze me. She spoke life into me, without even knowing the intricate details of all these very complex situations. I recognized and identified the pain, and she showed me what to do with it.

I checked into a hotel room that very afternoon. I spent hours feeling, crying, praying, eating, and writing. It was there that I found my fourth and final standard, and that would be to consult God before attaching myself to or dating anyone. I said a prayer of repentance and I asked God to reveal anything unlike him and to give me an open ear to hear him, to protect me. By the time I left the hotel the next morning, I was optimistic and excited for the future. I was motivated and I realized that something greater was available and forthcoming.

I made a personal commitment to better myself in every capacity. I created a plan that outlined my goals both long and short term. I took another vow of celibacy. I started going to the gym and envisioned myself becoming that person God created me to be. In a very short time frame, I changed my diet and picked up the hobby of cardio kickboxing, I lost over thirty pounds. My body, mind and spirit were changing. I had gotten good at kickboxing, learning the routines and how to land proper kicks and punches; but the ultimate lesson that I learned is that there's no hit like the one you don't see coming. I was on the brink of my most painful test - the knockout hit that would take me out.

Chapter Eight: Monkey See, Monkey Do

"When people are free to do as they please, they usually imitate each other."

— Eric Hoffer

Chapter Eight: Monkey see, Monkey do

One day my mother asked me whether I had ever dated someone who made me reconsider what I had claimed to want out of life, someone who made me want to get married. I immediately thought of Derrick, our longtime trusted family friend. I thought about all the times he had counseled me on my past relationships. I gave her a blank stare and slowly responded, "No."

There was a part, deep inside of me, that immediately thought of him. He had become my reason to guard my heart, because without any thought or question, I had broken my promises to God, relaxed my morals and let go of every standard I created. A year after leaving the relationship with Eric, I had encountered yet another someone who I thought could be trusted blindly and was beyond the rules.

Derrick had proclaimed for years that I would be the woman he would one day marry, remembering in detail our first initial introduction, that brought us both smiles, but today, I sat in sorrow. Silently I began to reminisce of the night that he and his daughter left Michigan. I began to reflect on the conversations we had promising that we would one day have a place of our own, similar or better than the one we were packing up. There were promises of how this was not goodbye, but, rather, see you later; but I realized that it had been over a year since I last saw them, and months since he and I had spoken.

As I sat in the car, I had to turn my head so that she wouldn't see the tears stream down my face. I wanted to tell her that being with the two of them was all I ever thought about. I wanted to say that I'd love nothing more than to be with him and raise a family. I wanted to cry to her about how my desire to grow old and reach the milestone of fifty-plus years of marriage was slowly fading; however, I couldn't acknowledge it, because it made it all too real for me.

I could share stories about all the times I've been caught daydreaming with a smile plastered across my face, only to be interrupted by reality. The absolute truth is that he had moved to Virginia and back into the home with his wife and kids. He left, without putting up any fight, and I was totally distraught. I couldn't breathe. I cried for days until my eyes were swollen shut and it all meant nothing.

For him, it all meant nothing, it just wasn't that deep - not even considered a relationship or dating. My friend, the man who had counseled me concerning not giving men too much credit, the man who told me to always guard my heart, the man I had talked about the future with and shared my body in the most intimate of ways with, didn't feel as though it was a big deal. Life had moved on for him, yet for me, my heart was frozen in time.

He left me feeling empty and alone. I needed him to be there emotionally at the very least, because logically I knew he could never be there physically. The United States Military had the final authority as to whether he'd be in my life. With divorce papers filed and a new enlistment contract signed, they gave him orders to relocate, making it mandatory that he be within 58 miles of his children.

Although legally I understood what was happening, it was hard to accept and process how fast everything transpired. I felt as if my world, my happiness had been stolen, forfeited. In a matter of days, he was gone, and just as fast as he was gone, it seemed like he just stopped caring. The sweet words "I Love You" and "Goodnight" became nonexistent. He FaceTimed me soon after leaving, from a bed (the same bed he shared with his wife). It didn't go well. He wasn't physically present or emotionally available for me and it felt like we were two worlds apart. He had been my friend for years, listening to the heartbreaking stories about me and other men, only to follow the exact same pattern.

I felt like an idiot! I am not sure how I did not see this coming, perhaps it was because of the level of friendship we shared. Since the first time we met in 2013, he had always said that I was who he was supposed to marry. For years he asked me when I would give him the time of day. I always brushed it off jokingly because I knew he was married. He would always say that this was the year, they were getting a divorce, but I always responded by telling him I wanted no part. I encouraged him to align himself spiritually under God so that his household would fall in order. He knew that there was a ministerial call on his life, yet he was so out of place and chaos had begun to break out inside of his marriage and home - division amongst not only him and his wife, but between his daughter and her stepmother (his wife), among other things. Yet, in the middle of their divorce, I selfishly involved myself.

This hurt was one of the worst pains in my life. One might believe that after being manipulated, humiliated and stalked, that nothing could top that experience, but I beg to differ. This one hurt me to the core because I purposely kept my distance from him. From the start I tried not to get too close, to build the most basic, almost shallow, of a friendship. For years I kept him at bay, never calling, texting or hanging out. I always deflected jokes and flirty remarks. I knew my intentions. I knew all along what I wanted, and he couldn't provide it. The thought of what I desired from him was there - if only he was available.

I tried to respect his wife, by only engaging in minimal and unavoidable interactions with him; yet, in the end I disrespected her, his family, myself and God, and, to a certain extent, Derrick assisted me. I get it, things were complicated. He was looking for a light and fluffy relationship with no commitment and what I offered up was heavy and full of obligation, I was ready for love. I was ready to learn, build and grow together, ready to give, change, restructure and conquer it all - with him.

He was one of the good guys ... but aren't they all? In each of them I could pick out perfections. Each one was perfect in his own right ... perfect in their ability to shake up my life and leave me questioning my morals. I willingly broke every rule when it came to him. I shared with him pieces of my body, heart, and mind that had never been exposed to anyone else, as we discussed the turmoil of my last relationship with Eric. For the first time, I had encountered a man who served the same God I did. He reached parts of me spiritually that had never been discovered by another man, with his ability to pray, fast, and worship with me. I loved him deeply, mostly because I desired to love him.

In early March of 2017, I received a phone call from my sister, letting me know that Derrick would be stopping by my mom's business. I hadn't seen him since his father's funeral the year before, so I was excited to see how he was doing. He made a joke about the two of us getting together when he arrived, as always.

I sarcastically responded, "Whenever you get a divorce."

I guess the joke was on me, because he replied by saying that the papers had been filed in February, that in January she took his son and moved to Virginia. I was in shock. I briefly reasoned with myself that this was fair game, and I didn't have any part of the blame. I had never crossed any lines with him. I thought to myself, "Their marriage didn't end because of me," and, "Hey, this is a good man. I don't owe her anything."

So naturally, my next question to him was, "So when are we going on a date?"

That same night, we stayed on the phone all night, talking, singing and giggling like teenagers. Everything had always been natural between us, but this was different. We talked about God, the same god. He sang my spirit happy with gospel songs and we preached scriptures and sermons. The heart I had been working so hard to guard over the past year was easily accessed. My guard was completely down when it came to Derrick. We went on a couple dates that week, and I even stayed over at his house. He was the perfect gentleman, keeping a respectable distance, and not focusing too much on physical touch.

As usual, with all my stories, turmoil soon followed. I learned that he was also talking to one of my college friends, Ava. She called me and shared that the two of them had been hanging out and sleeping together over the past three weeks. I told him, as any good honest women would, that it was fun while it lasted; that I'd love for our friendship to continue, but I wasn't the type of girl to date behind my friends. I asked him to keep his distance, and to end our communication. As always, things had been too good to be true.

Two days later he showed up at my mom's building, asking me to forgive him for not being upfront, and to reconsider. He argued that he never thought I would ever take him seriously, and that he just didn't know how to tell me. Under the counsel of my sisters and several other friends, yet against my better judgement, I forgave him with the expectancy that the relationship between the two of them would end. Sadly, I soon learned that there were several romantic relationships that he was still trying to purge from his life. It started with Ava, but soon I learned of another, and more about the unfinished business with his wife.

As the story goes, divorce papers were filed in February and there was a waiting period of 180 days because they had a child. I'm not sure how much of that is true, because I never saw the finalized copies, nor do I believe they exist. To this day I believe they are still married and living together. I often wonder if I got caught in the middle of a mid-life crisis, and I was the scapegoat. Nevertheless, what I did gain from this ordeal was a broken heart, shattered to pieces and frozen in time. It's been years, and the only things about this that still pains me is my relationship with his daughter.

Kayla was 12 when he and I started seeing each other. I had known her for years, so she easily embraced me when she saw her dad and I were spending a lot of time together, calling me her stepmother. She had a desire to have the bond with me that she couldn't have with his wife, her real stepmother. I spent weeks with this young girl, bonding, doing hair, makeup, nails, shopping, lunch and, of course, plenty of girl talk. We were close, and it's no doubt that my connection with her was more genuine than the one I shared with him. Although I knew I was not her mother, she allowed me to feel what it was like to have a young child look up to me, one to trust me for advice and direction, someone to admire me and for me to protect.

She is an amazing child, with a very bright future. She is a leader, and that was something I told her all the time. We talked about their family, and how she wanted to move to from Kentucky, where she lived with her birth mom, to Michigan with her dad, and that she felt like her stepmother did not like her. We were close, it's possible that I spent more time with her during visits than Derrick did. I cried so hard when we dropped her off at the airport because her time with us had ended so quickly.

He promised that she'd return in three weeks, when school ended for the summer, but what none of us were expecting was for our time to be drastically cut short, due to his relocation. I never imagined that there would come a time when I would talk to her without speaking to him, and that I would travel hundreds of miles to visit her, only to be told I could not see her.

For over a year, I cried and stood in disbelief of how rapidly life had changed. One moment he was here, and I was living a blind life, pretending as though everything was perfect, and the next I was questioning God on how this could happen, why this "good thing" was denied to me.

I now recognize that this short-term ordeal was all set-in motion by God to save me from myself. Again, I had wandered into a situation I had no business being in, and God had to rescue me. As quickly as it began, it ended. By June 13, 2017, he was gone. He packed up his apartment and left me with a hole in my heart. With less than two weeks' notice, he had received orders to relocate to Virginia, and he moved back into the house with his wife. What once seemed so secure, I could feel was desolate. Conversations changed in context and in availability. If I spoke to him at all, it was briefly. The promises of returning to Michigan to visit soon, changed to, "I'm not sure when, or if, I'll make it back."

Arguments begin to arise, and It became clear just how illegitimate our relationship was. Family pictures from vacations, a Father's Day post and first day of school pictures made it perfectly and painfully clear that he had a life outside of me - one where I had no place, or entitlement. Everything that I received, his attention, time, gifts and temporal words to make the pain go away, was stolen. I had involved myself in a covenant that was sacred to God, and oh was I feeling the wrath of my sin. Resentment, jealousy, bitterness and torment were the least of what I felt. There was a strong distaste, a hatred for their union, for their family. I felt she didn't deserve him or desire him. My heart had become a nasty place, unavailable to anybody.

I had involved myself in their marriage because I had a lack of respect for other women and for myself. The idea or notion that I didn't owe her, his wife, anything resonated with me for years to come. The truth is, I didn't owe her anything, I owed her everything, I owed God everything. I owed myself everything. I had become yet again, everything I despised. The least that I could have given her, out of respect for God and her family, was the ability to conquer battles and challenges with her husband without the involvement of another woman making it more difficult. I had been hurt more times than I could count, yet here I was hurting another woman.

I never once considered what it was like for her to be on the other side of him, as he FaceTimed another woman with headphones on, talking in our version of a code, as if she wasn't smart enough to know. I never once considered that perhaps the barriers that existed behind her and his daughter became greater because she had placed someone else in the stepmother space in her heart and had written her off as the step-monster. I was wrong, and the only thing I could do to make it right was cut ties, but I still knew all too well, that spiritually it wasn't that simple.

Chapter Nine:
Plenty of Fish…Just Not You!

Now My Dream of Finding Love Can Be Crushed More Efficiently and in the Privacy of My Own Home."

-Tammera 21

Chapter Nine: Plenty of Fish…Just Not You!

I was finally at a point where I thought I was over it. My standards for dating were at an all-time low, after another heartbreaking blow. I decided that I had nothing to lose, and possibly everything to gain, by trying online dating. Out of a mixture of boredom and desperation, I decided to create two online dating profiles. I reasoned that at the very least I'd have a chance to hold a conversation with an adult of the opposite sex, and that it couldn't make my love life any bleaker than its current state.

The first profile I created was on Soul Swipe. I thought to myself, "It's simple enough, swipe right or left based on whether you'd date them." If you have any matches, they will notify you, and, if not, you'll never know. I had more matches than I expected. Men soon filled my notifications, giving me the option of picking who I'd be interested in responding to. There were several guys that held my attention long enough for me to give them my number.

The first fit the description of being my "type." He was tall, dark and handsome with nice teeth, and an athletic build. From his photos I could tell he had style, dressing primarily in business professional attire. There was one problem, though, he preferred to date transgender women. Rather than question whether he assumed I was a transgender, I just cut communication and blocked him.

I spoke with a second guy on several occasions, but everything inside screamed for me to distance myself from him. The taunting similarities between him and Eric were just too strong, and I knew there would be trouble ahead. I quickly realized that Soul Swipe was not my forte and moved on to my second online dating experience, Plenty of Fish.

I had hundreds of men flood my inbox with messages from the moment I uploaded my first picture. It was flattering to be admired by so many men in such a short amount of time, however, it quickly became overbearing. Each had their own story of how beautiful I was, how they couldn't believe I was on a dating site and how they wanted to get to know me. I believe I made it through the first twenty profiles before I got overwhelmed. I decided to remove my photos and stop responding to new inbox messages. I only respond to a few of the old messages and gave my phone number to one, a young man named Shawn who had a love of God, music, anime, battle rap and learning. He was a psychology major who drove for Uber on the side. He lived alone and owned his own vehicle. He was the only prospect who had a conversation worth entertaining, our mutual interest in God.

Our conversations were so natural, we didn't have to force anything. We talked about the Bible, family, dreams, goals and what we wanted out of the future. We talked for weeks on the phone, learning about each other. Everything was perfect, except for one thing, he didn't desire a relationship. This was a cycle I knew all too well, yet I continued to communicate with him in an effort to have someone present in my life. If I have learned one thing from my dating thus far, it's that we don't really know what we want until we want it. I had been told before by men that they weren't interested in a relationship, only to have them fall over and spill their hearts out to me. So, while it was just conversation, I allowed it to be.

Weeks went on and we began to learn more about each other. We shared our upbringing, shortcomings, and, eventually, some of our darkest secrets. He was a very nice guy and he was honest to a fault at times. Shawn was vulnerable about the challenges that he faced within his family and many intimate battles he fought physically, financially, emotionally, spiritually and mentality.

To summarize it all, he was a loner. He didn't have any family, or friends. There was no one present in his life to support his dreams. He lived a very lonely life for many years, absent of people, but he was still filled with a sense of purpose. He held onto his faith by a mire thread, desiring for God to prove him wrong. His heart had been broken by his first love, and he no longer believed in pure love. He had waited on God to bring true love into his life. As the years continued to pass, his faith weakened, and he was ready to throw it all away - everything that he had prayed for, everything that he had saved.

Selfishly I thought, "Me too! This is going to be perfect; God has brought us together."

I knew that I had the capacity to love him, and I set my mind on building with him and being a friend to him, although my heart was never really into it. I loved him as a friend, and I desired to be there for him. He had asked me to give him time, to adjust to the thought of being in a relationship, promising that it would come.

With both of us letting our guards down, we began to spend more time together. I stayed over at his place three to four nights out of the week. He'd buy me gifts and we would go out on dates. I learned that he was a virgin and we soon made several attempts to become sexually active with one another, yet each time we failed because of his inability to perform. The closer we got to one another, the worse our communication and progress became. Finally, he got to a point to where he was completely honest with me about how he felt.

While I was attempting to gain an understanding about why this was happening between us, he bluntly shared that he could never be attracted to my body. He said that he preferred the slim-thick body style, and that I was too big to please him sexually. The conversation continued, as he went on to say that he was disgusted by my vagina, that it was repulsive. I was distraught, and in efforts to preserve my self-esteem, I quickly got on the speaker phone to call Derrick and began questioning him about the appearance and smell of my vagina. Although this helped to reassure me that no one else had ever had this problem, this of course became very problematic, causing another argument between Shawn and I.

Needless to say, this ended my period of online dating. I never returned to his home after the incident. In just three months the entire ordeal did a number on my already staggeringly low self-esteem. I found myself reflecting a lot in the weeks following the end of the relationship. I had begun to question whether there was something wrong with me that made me unworthy of love. I questioned why I was not enough, not only for him, but it seemed like for anyone I had ever dated.

I thought about how I had progressed with my weight. I was kickboxing at the time, and weighed in at a toned 167 pounds, down more than 50 pounds from my 218-pound climax in 2011. I began to reflect on the other lifestyle changes I had made, as I had been a consistent vegetarian for four years. I knew how I had progressed with managing my weight, and I realized that I could not allow someone to project what they believed I should be onto me, or, moreso, how I should view myself.

I had worked hard to fix everything that could've been considered an issue. I had been down this road before, changing my outer appearance to accommodate the man I was dating; even to the extent of getting braces. I changed my weight, my sense of fashion and my hairstyle multiple times to make others happy. I changed everything that I thought could make me undesirable, even down to hobbies and habits, and still, it wasn't enough. I wasn't enough. Regardless of how much I weighed, how long or short my hair was, and regardless of how I dressed, there was always going to be someone who did not like it. There was always someone one who did not desire me.

For the first time ever, I could clearly identify the fight I had been engaging in all these years. I fought not with flesh and blood, but with spiritual wickedness in high places (Ephesians 6:2). I realized that the battle I was fighting was within my own mind, rather than external. The battle wasn't with the women I considered to be prettier than me, nor was it with the men who didn't feel I was enough, but it was with the way I viewed myself. I did not view myself as being worthy of God's promises, grace and provisions, therefore, I gave in to the identity that Satan desired for me to believe. Rather than hold to the ideal that I was created in the image of God, and adopted as a child of God, making me a joint heir with Christ; I settled for seeing myself through the paradigm that the enemy had led me through.

Chapter Ten: Beneath the Surface

"From birth, man carries the weight of gravity on his shoulders. He is bolted to earth. But man has only to sink beneath the surface and he is free."

-Jacques Yves Cousteau

Chapter Ten: Beneath the Surface

It had been a solid six years of being single. Notice I said single - just single - not to say that I went six years without sex. A large portion of that time was set aside to celibacy, however. Single as in no one has felt it necessary to commit their life to me under God, or even attempt to build something remotely close to being real. From 2011 to 2017, I had wasted time with John, Eric, Derrick, and Shawn and none of them had considered me worthy of commitment. Let's face it; it is quite possible that it has been longer than six years of being single, because truth be told, I was both physically and emotionally checked out of my last relationship for its last two years, experiencing the back and forth of long-term breakups and the "I don't know what I want" phase.

At first, I wasn't opposed to being single, and to a certain extent I'm still not. I do, however, wonder if I gave away a vibe that told men that I am emotionally withdrawn and damaged. I didn't trust them, and as much as I wanted to, I didn't know how to love blindly. In all honesty, I had a reason for my trust issues: my birth father never loved me, my first love became an atheist and was verbally abusive concerning the God I love, and the next man I opened up to was emotionally unable to meet in a place conducive for us to grow - and that was just the beginning.

If I were to go into detail about what I experienced as a child with my mother, aunts and older cousins - both male and female - it's safe to say I've seen enough to deter any rational person from desiring love. Strangely enough, it did not. The crazy thing is, I thought and dreamt of falling in love all the time. There was a part of me that secretly hoped that true, fearless, unchanging, relentless, breathtaking love still existed. I wanted to get to experience it firsthand, but if not, at least have the opportunity to view it in its rarest, and realest form - one day bringing forth life and becoming a mother.

I used to dream of a love where both parties are so lost in each other that your sense of time stands still, yet the world passes by, leaving you without a care. I used to dream of a love where you get lost in someone's eyes, forgetting that pain, poverty, or evil exist; the love that creates an unidentifiable melody each time you lock eyes. Although I've almost felt that "drop everything and run kind of love"- like the kind we see at the end of movies. The love that makes us forsake everything and chase after our soulmate; its close, but no cigar.

Years later, at the age of 28, I still sought after that "Can't eat, can't sleep, reach for the stars over the moon, world series" kind of love. I often questioned whether that is the reason I never experienced genuine love, but only a soiled fragment of what it should entail. Perhaps my desire for it was too great, too real. Maybe I would lose my purpose in the love of someone else. I'd like to believe that I would not throw away my future goals and dreams because I fell in love, yet at times running away and becoming a tree-hugging hippie doesn't sound too bad. It sounds free and deep. It's intriguing.

There was an episode of ABC's "Scandal" where Cyrus Beene (Jeff Perry) gave advice to Oliva Pope (Kerry Washington) concerning her relationship with President Fitzgerald "Fitz" Grant (Tony Goldwyn). He said that "some men aren't meant to be happy, they're meant to be great." I was captivated by that statement. In her sacrificial act of pushing her feelings to the side for Fitz to successfully complete his presidency, Olivia denied what was thought to be her one true love, however messy and toxic it may have been. I remember thinking to myself that perhaps those with a greater ability to create meaningful global and social change are left with no ability to share their life with anything or anyone else. Maybe my love of humanity, my love for God's people, is meant to be the deepest depth to my experience.

A part of me wondered why I was fought so much to love men who had no desire to be who they lead me to believe they were. My best friend Nicole would say it's because of my "type". She says that I like educated men, with a past - one who has gotten his life together but is still a little rough around the edges. It's not hard for me to believe that this is true considering my history, but I think a more accurate depiction would be that I've often desired men who are outside of God's will because I had never fully submitted to God. Despite all my praying, fasting, teaching, preaching and leading, there was a part deep inside of me that desired to live as the captain of this ship. I was still using my own logic to determine what my life could, should and would be like. The only problem was, under my own navigation, I had run this ship into a major iceberg. It was sinking right before my eyes. I had begun to navigate with a sense of recklessness, with no boundaries, limitations or standards to anchor me.

What I could not see was that underneath the surface, under the smiles, jokes and laughter was a girl who was slowly dying - not physically, but spiritually. I kept allowing relationships to chip away at my mind, body and spirit. The men I attached to my soul created wounds deep within my being, leaving scars that neither stitches nor staples could hold together. Each time I grew weaker, allowing men who were offering less than what my standard was to access more of me.

I was desperately searching for something that had been with me all along, God. I desired a tangible presence, someone to ease my pain, make everything better in the midst of life's chaos. I wanted someone to hold me and tell me everything would be alright; someone to lie to me, as we stood face to face, telling me everything I wanted to hear, because I didn't love myself enough to look in the mirror and acknowledge the ugliness of my sin. After each break up, I would reminisce over old pictures, letters and memories. I would stand in the mirror and look at my swollen eyes, my red face, raw nose and messy hair. I'd wonder how these men could hurt me when I had loved them so much, the truth is I should have been asking myself those same questions. How could I hurt God, when he loved me so much? How could I fail to hold on to the truths that God had already shared with me and believe that I was worthy of his protection and provision?

Time after time, he had shown me that he thought I was worthy. He had protected me from hurt, harm and danger, only allowing me to experience enough heat, that I'd know to get out of the kitchen. How could I not heed his warning? What about God's broken heart? Each time I laid in bed with these men, I took his spirit with me. I allowed these men to contaminate God's Temple. I told God each time that I chose other men over my relationship with him, that he wasn't good enough, when all he ever tried to tell me was that I was. I'd soon grasp this concept. The only question was, "Was I too late?"

Chapter Eleven: Choose YOU this Day …

"And if it seem evil unto you to serve the Lord, choose you this day whom ye will serve; whether the gods which your fathers served that were on the other side of the flood, or the gods of the Amorites, in whose land ye dwell: but as for me and my house, we will serve the Lord."

Joshua 24:15 King James Version (KJV)

Chapter Eleven: Choose YOU this Day …

It was on a Tuesday in February 2018 when God gave me the ultimatum of whether I would live or die. I had been called into my doctor's office for a biopsy of my cervix. Yet again, my test results had returned with abnormal cell changes was a possibility that they were cancerous. I felt discomfort and soreness as I laid on the table, the physician scraping my cervix to collect samples, but the discomfort and soreness did not compare to the agony of my past.

During those next few moments, every sexual encounter I'd ever experienced crossed the threshold of my mind. I thought about my first love and the day I lost my virginity. In regret, I shed a tear for how naive I was to accept Darrin back, after he had left me and slept with other women, not once, but twice exposing and infecting me with sexually transmitted infections. I remembered all the ways of escape God had provided me and how, in my own lustful flesh, I returned to danger.

I pondered on how life had changed since being with John. The situationship and college had ended, and, at least in my everyday life, I was no longer labeled a groupie. While I was grateful for the release from taunting, bullying and legal issues that came from fighting, I thought I'd give up the entire encounter with him if it meant I could have my reputation, and relationships with my peers restored.

Tears flooded my face as I thought about the physical, mental and spiritual attacks I faced from Eric, who was spiritually lost. I thought about how I was once treated as though I was his property, that he declared ownership over. Completely exposed and vulnerable, I questioned whether the doctor could smell the stench of my sin, whether he could see the wounds left behind after they had all come and gone. I thought of Derrick, the imposter, in the form of a friend, who had hurt me deeply and how reckless it was for me to be sexually intimate with a married man. I laid there in disgust at how I had let myself and my standards go, desperately wanting to be released from my ties with him.

I questioned how much of the spiritual and physical attacks I'd experienced were rooted in my sexual relationships with men, and the spiritual ties they shared with me - and probably hundreds of other women. I felt sick to my stomach. I had always been one to get tested regularly and use protection with non-committed partners, however, on this day, fear set in. It was a fear that froze me, paralyzed me and made me not want to feel anything - joy or pain.

I decided that day that I would not feel anything. In an effort to numb my emotions, I ate a piece of a medical marijuana muffin, in hope of not feeling anything. Within a matter of hours, I felt as though I was losing my head. The enemy began to talk to me and tell me, tell me that I would never be the same.

I began to feel as though my brain was swelling. I had an urge to take off my clothes as my body began to overheat. I could not breathe, and my body began to spasm. I could feel my eyes going in and out; I felt as if I was about to have a seizure. I knew that I was literally dying, yet I could not utter words to get help.

I mumbled to my cousin that I needed to go to the hospital, and he reasoned with me that I was just high. He instructed me to go outside and cool off. As I walked onto the porch, I could feel myself about to collapse.

I heard God say, "Choose this day whom you will serve."

I responded, "You."

With all the strength left inside of me, I ran into my mother's room. When I arrived there, I saw that she was already praying, and the Holy Spirit had already revealed to her what I was going through. She grabbed me, placing one hand on my heart and another on my head and I fell to the floor. I remember her praying over me. As she began to intercede over me, God began to tell me "No more, no more turning back."

I soon began regurgitating everything that I had digested that day. Over the next couple of weeks, my body went through different changes. My eye would still twitch, and my body had different spasms, but as I submitted to God these issues disappeared.

Over the next couple of months, God began to minister to me in my study time with him. He called me to a place of complete spiritual detox, unlike anything that I had ever experienced before. He gave me three steps. The first, was to eliminate everything and everybody as a part of the spiritual detox. During this time, I separated myself from everyone and everything. I eliminated all my social media accounts, because the last thing I needed was a reminder of how I didn't measure up to society's standards. I put distance between myself and all of my friends. I made it an active practice to not use my cell phone as much and to not be around anything or anyone that wasn't Christ-centered. I wanted to eliminate all the toxins that had drawn a wedge between God and I.

When choosing what to unplug, I left it completely up to the Holy Spirit, rather than reason with myself, like I had in the past. This time I offered everything up to God: friends, family, business, and anything else he desired to be in control over. I must admit that I did not fully understand the magnitude of what this submission would cost me, but I wouldn't change the outcome for anything. Over the next few months I lost many of my closest friends. This put me in a very uncomfortable and unfamiliar place, because people who had been with me for decades, men and women who I loved like brothers and sisters, could not take this journey with me. It became even more apparent that the more I connected to the source, God, the more alone I felt. The spiritual elevation process often requires separation. It's not because you are better, or holier, but rather so that you can get into a place where you can hear only God, not the ideas and opinions of others.

This leads me to the second step of my detox, which was to tune everything out. There are times when loneliness lingers and I desire to run back to the life I'm familiar with, but the woman God is creating must be birthed. Her purpose must be fulfilled, and her calling is worth more than the temporal feelings of familiarity. Choose where God is taking you over everything and everybody.

At the time my thoughts had begun to work against me, telling me that I had been down this road before and that I knew how it ended. My rational mind and the enemy told me that I would eventually go back to the life of sin. I had to constantly feed my spirit the word of God. I would read the word, pray, and just ask God to keep me. I was one hundred percent vulnerable with God concerning my fears and desires.

I clung to the scriptures, using them to fight off the thoughts I had that were contrary to the word of God. This helped me to trace my emotions to their root cause. For example, if fear was arising because of my past, I would begin to speak that God had not given me the spirit of fear, but of power, love, and a sound mind. I would rebuke my thoughts and speak to my mind, commanding it to be renewed and transformed in Christ Jesus.

The final and (never-ending) step was to draw into God. I buried myself, my heart and my desires in his word. I learned what he thought about me, and I asked him to reveal specific things about my future that would keep me on track. I asked him for a confirmation question, a question tailor-made to my future, that would let me know that courtship was acceptable. A question that gave me insight, letting me know that the man I would encounter could be trusted with my purpose.

I began to prepare for what I was asking God to do in my life. I wanted a husband, I desired marriage, so I began to study singleness, courtship and marriage. My prayer was that God would eliminate anything inside of me that was unlike him, to help me see myself and his people how he does. I asked him to help me to love how he loves and forgive how he forgives.

A couple months after beginning my detox, my dad tapped me on my shoulder at a Saturday service and told me I was up to preach. Ironically, this would be the same service one of my longtime best friends from college, Robert, would attend. I spoke about being on a spiritual detox, and soon he'd share that God had been dealing with him in a similar manner. I had always been protective over my close friends, so when he told me that he had been going to church and taking a class on spiritual gifts, I felt compelled to know more about where he was worshiping and his learning.

The next day, I walked into Faith Tabernacle Church in Highland Park, Michigan. My life would never be the same. From that day on,

Robert and I prayed, studied and talked about God together. We attended my church on Saturdays and his church on Sundays. We also created an accountability fellowship for young adults called The Consecration Walk, where we encouraged other young adults to do just as we were - chase after God wholeheartedly.

About two months into attending Faith Tabernacle, he and I signed up to participate in an inner healing and deliverance service. During this service, people were paired with a spiritual counselor. The counselors ask a series of questions, and, through the direction of the Holy Spirit and prayer, trace the root of the issues you are facing. We were given a card and told to write down the things we sought deliverance from. I wrote past relationships, trauma, daddy issues and eating disorders, attempting to stay in a comfortable conversation zone by giving vague topics.

I was extremely guarded going into the service, so I prayed and asked God to place me with one of the two elders present, that I was familiar with. As you can probably guess, that didn't happen. I was instructed to go over to another elder, who I had only had a brief introduction to. She was a very nice woman, extremely beautiful and well spoken. I thought to myself, "Yeah right lady, there's no way I'm pouring out my heart and being completely vulnerable; I don't really know you."

She began to ask me questions, and I gave responses that were very direct. After asking me about three questions, she said, "Something isn't right." She then stopped speaking and started praying. After praying, she asked me, "What did you come here for; because I came for deliverance." Before I could say anything, she began to pray a spirit of adultery off me.

As the tears began to flow, I sat in front of her completely open and vulnerable. I could feel the spirit lift off me as we prayed. I felt clarity inside of my mind, and I felt strength. From that day forward, I never had the urge or desire to run back to the relationships or situationships I once yearned for. Never again did I speak to, date, or engage with, Derrick, the married man who I had been emotionally attached to for the past year.

Chapter Twelve: The Promise

"For I know the thoughts that I think toward you, saith the Lord, thoughts of peace, and not of evil, to give you an expected end."

Jeremiah 29:11 King James Version (KJV)

Chapter Twelve: The Promise

It had been almost five months of fasting, praying, disconnecting myself from social media and the rest of the world and hiding myself in God. My best friend had been right there alongside me, cleaning out his house and recalibrating his mind. As our fast continued and The Consecration Walk grew, people begin to inquire about my relationship status and how my best friend and I were of the opposite sex, yet able to be platonic friends. They were in complete disbelief. I shared with them that I was waiting on God, not dating anyone, but, as you can imagine, these questions soon changed from, "How are you all friends?," to "We don't believe that you all are friends."

Our status or lack thereof had become the elephant in every room, whether it be amongst family, church family, or even co-workers. To say the least, we thought that everyone, our parents and pastors included were being awkward. After church one afternoon, amid another conversation of whether we were dating or not, I decided to clear the air. It was my fear that other people might make him uncomfortable, or even perhaps that we were missing something that everyone else was able to notice. So, on our way to brunch in early July of 2018, I asked him whether he liked me. His response was that he was going to ask me the exact same thing.

He agreed that if we were to ever date, we would need the Lord to make it very clear, because we did not want to destroy a friendship of over a decade by moving outside of God's will. He responded by telling me to pray to God about it, and that he would do the same. That same evening, I prayed to God and enquired of his plan, I asked him to protect my heart. I asked him to equip Robert and I to hear from him, and to cover our friendship.

Tuesday, Aug. 21, 2018

As I laid in my bed, in the middle of the night, I experienced an awakening by the Holy Spirit. This wasn't a new experience for me, because God often woke me from my sleep to give me messages or directions, or to have me begin intercessory prayer. So, on this night, like many others, I created a note inside of my cell phone. I began to write as the Holy Spirit directed me:

> *A bond that was created in heaven, cultivated by God himself. The beautiful thing about being Handcrafted is that you've been carefully created with precision to serve a certain task, purpose, or for the fulfillment of a need. Every detail slowly aligned and customized to perfection making it unique and one of a kind. Handcrafted items are normally derived of the best and most durable materials so that it can withstand its need for use. As the handcrafted item is being created the artist develops a set of experiences and memories to go along with the work. They can remember the good, bad, joy, and pain as each area of their work tells a story. Time is perhaps the most*

precious resource of its creation. The duration of the labor adds more to its value. The more time it takes to build the work of art, the greater the appreciation. Handcrafted items aren't created easily, or rushed, but rather with careful consideration of its function and inside of a protected environment.

Handcrafted items are better items than those that have been massed produced. This is a specialized customization, that takes time to build. It isn't an overnight process, but the durability will last beyond anything imaginable. They are Antiques; collectibles, that increase in value as they age. Showing their experience and maturity as their collective beauty adds to shape to what once was one dimensional.

Even after this word, I was unsure of where Robert was in his praying for direction, so I began to pray and journal. I asked God to give me patience and to keep me from moving out of order. As confirmation that our relationship was handcrafted by God, I asked God to give Robert that same word, and I promised him that I wouldn't move forward until he did just that. I continued to journal and document prophecies and revelations.

When I think about the dimensions of our friendship, and how they are about to change I get nervous. Please know that I would never intentionally hurt you or do something that puts us into a bad position. Know that

I'm willing to be your friend and love you even when I feel like I don't like you. I'm willing to expose my flaws, fears, bite my tongue, and fight alongside you behind God to protect what he's given us. I promise to fight to be the best version of myself and a helpmate because I know it's what you deserve and it's what God desires. You deserve someone who desires to love you as you love them how Christ loves the church, one who will submit to you as unto the Lord. Someone who enjoys the opportunity to make you smile and wants nothing more than to see you evolve into the man God has called you to be. One who prays for your soul, protects your interest, and defends your characters knowing without a doubt your hearts true intent.

I recognize that hard times will come, but I'm believing God for his promises of this handcrafted relationship that can withstand anything that comes its way. Created of a material capable of weathering any storm. No blizzard, hurricane, or tsunami great enough to conquer what God has put together. When I think about what it means for God to have handcrafted us, I am in awe of the amazing story our friendship tells. Honored that he thought enough of me to create such a beautiful soul to coincide with mine. Humbled by his thoughtfulness and protection. Floored by his mercy and grace, for I don't deserve his kindness.

It's amazing to me the things God has shown me concerning you. How fast life is moving, and I can't think of another person I'd rather share a seat with on this rollercoaster we call life. Someone who's sure to not only lift my hands but also my smile. Someone who is certain to sing when we're falling from the sky. A man who will cover me in fasting and praying. Make me laugh until I cry, and one whom I can share my darkest flaws and secrets.

I'm honored it's you. You make it easy to love you. As I write this, you know nothing about how I really feel. I've been writing this letter for months as I wait for God to give you this word. This waiting although frustrating and lonely at times has taught me so much about myself. I've learned to keep my hands, words, and tantrums to myself. I've learned to respect your ability to hear from God. I've learned to respect you, and that you are not something or someone for me to manipulate to get my way. There have been many times when other women both young and old have suggested that I do or say certain things to get a response out of you. I respect you too much to twist your arm, maneuver, or trick you into something. More than anything I've desired to keep this pure and to allow God and you to lead in whatever way he sees fit. It was hard for me to keep my mouth closed especially when God was teaching me or revealing certain things about you to me. When I could see how purpose, prophecies, and callings were being fulfilled and I couldn't share but only pray. I learned that I can love you, but I must solely rely on God- regardless because we belong to him.

Some of the hardest times to deal with, were when I wanted to show affection. Hold your hand, touch you even in a non-sexual way, but I was not allowed. It was moments like that, when I would pull out my phone or computer to write. Knowing that one day you will read this, and hopefully appreciate how much it meant to me to ensure that both you and God were honored. I never want to step out of place. When we were in South Africa on our way back from Pretoria, I wanted to hold your hand, but I couldn't. Perhaps it was the music they were playing, or my emotions going for it being my special time of the month, but I felt a desire to be closer to you. For the first time, it really scared me that you might not feel the same. I used that time to talk to God and ask him to make it clear. I wanted there to be no doubt or insecurity concerning you.

Oct. 7, 2019, Johannesburg, South Africa

We had just finished packing up our hotel room and moving our luggage into the lobby of the hotel, just before checking out. We still had to attend church, but we were about to take an 18-hour flight back to the United States, one day before my birthday. We also needed to find some authentic, handcrafted clothing to take back with us. It had become the entire theme of our trip, we had searched multiple malls, shops and small village stores looking for authentic African clothing. Robert had complained that he didn't want mass-produced clothing, that he would prefer handcrafted attire and I had missed every connection.

I was so grateful that he had traveled all the way to South Africa with me, in awe of how blessed we were to be in the Motherland to serve God. We had a great time indeed, with both of us being able to minister at different churches. As one might imagine, it was bittersweet as we waited in the lobby for transportation to our final church service, with a trip to the airport and a return flight to follow. There I stood, taking pictures of the waterfall and fountain, which contained the most beautiful exotic fish.

In the background I could hear him fussing at me about not paying attention to details. After a minute or two of him fussing, I turned around to see him on one knee, holding a small black box, which contained a very beautiful diamond ring. I stood there in awe and smiled as Robert told me, the details of the ring. He shared that it was an heirloom, once belonging to his mother. She told him to give it to the woman he would spend the rest of his life with. He said that through prayer, God had shown him I was the answer to his prayers; that we had been handcrafted by God. There was no doubt in my mind whether this was ordained by God, there was no fear of being unequally yoked, and for once in my life I was certain that the man I had given my heart too could be trusted. God had given me full permission to enter courtship.

As I walked toward him with tears streaming down my face, he embraced me with open arms. Within seconds I leaned back, to get a good look at him, still in total disbelief of what was occurring, I held onto him tighter. With a smile he told me, "I would really love to kiss you right now, but we are going to do this God's way.

I smiled and nodded in agreement as my thoughts drifted back to the pink conference room at my parent's place, where sitting at the computer after reading Heather Lindsey's Blog, I had prayed for proof. I prayed to God years ago, asking whether a woman with a flawed sinful past, a heartbroken one, who did not look like the American standard of beauty, or have the best education, could ever find real love. I asked whether we too, qualified for the promise? I asked him whether stories like this: fairy tales of true love, courtship, celibacy and holiness were available for women like me? In that very moment, God answered, “ABSOLUTELY!”

LIGHTING UP
THE DARK PLACES:
THE TESTIMONY OF
ROBERT J. JOHNS

Available at
amazon

www.ingramcontent.com/pod-product-compliance
Lightning Source LLC
LaVergne TN
LVHW091006080826
845145LV00003B/1156
9781734194845